Pearson's Canal Comp[anion]

KENNET & AV[ON]

and the River Thames from Oxford to Brentford

Published by Central Waterways Supplies
of Rugby. Tel/fax 01788 546692
Copyright: Michael Pearson - All rights reserved.
Second edition 2007. ISBN 978 0 9 5491167 6

Tillerman

I must say I've enjoyed returning to the Kennet & Avon and middle Thames to work on the second edition of this guide, and in doing so taking the opportunity to extend coverage of the Thames downstream to Brentford where it links with Pearson's Canal Companion to the Oxford & Grand Union Canals; thus offering complete coverage of the so-called 'Thames Ring'. In any case second editions, like second innings, always offer the guide compiler, like the batsman, the chance to do a bit better, to notice anything missed the first time, to fine tune the prose, to turn, as it were, undignified dashes between the wickets into firmly struck boundaries.

And the odd thing is, the older I get, the more in tune with the south I feel. Like Belloc before me, I am beginning to find the Midlands, 'sodden and unkind', and when 'I light my lamp in the evening ... the great hills of the South Country come back into my mind'. I had forgotten an early cognisance with the Kennet & Avon, a day spent in the illustrious company of Denys Hutchings on a whistle-stop tour of the canal before it was fully restored. In the cool interior of the Barge Inn at Honey Street, mellowed by Usher's bitter, it was impossible not to be bowled over by his contagious enthusiasm. And even then - it must have been circa 1979 - full restoration of the Kennet & Avon seemed such a just and worthy cause - a canal crusade if ever there was one - that you wondered why it was taking so long, and why the responsibility lay with well-meaning individuals like Denys as opposed to central government to have this great inland waterway reconstituted, rendering once again the facility of a broad-beam link between London and Bristol. But then you remembered that it was a peculiarly British trait to create and to then destroy or abandon; a childish facility for making toys then breaking them.

I suppose it is a miracle that navigation of the Thames was never abandoned in the manner of the Severn above Stourport and the Trent above Shardlow. What saved the Thames, following the demise of commercial trade towards the end of the 19th Century, was leisure; a Victorian and Edwardian paroxysm of pleasure boating that barely abated despite the rude interruption of two world wars. Decline set in as the general public got it into their heads that more fun could be derived from driving along increasingly crowded roads than boating on the river. In this, as in many other aspects of modern life, they were deluded. Cheap foreign holidays deflected further from the Thames' traditional appeal, but of late there has been something of a renaissance in public perception of the river's regenerative powers; not least with the opening of the Thames Path National Trail together with increased use of the river by canal-based craft joining it from the Kennet & Avon, Oxford and Grand Union canals. It will inevitably be amongst this latter category that this new guide finds its broadest readership. I trust they will enjoy exposure to the landscape and history of the Royal Thames as much as I have done.

Michael Pearson

UK-BOATING *holidays*

If you are looking for a boating holiday you need look no further

3

The Kennet & Avon Canal

1 RIVER AVON NAVIGATION

ENVY the lucky boater who has to begin or end their voyage in the superbly atmospheric setting of Bristol's Floating Harbour: of course it's the vessels which 'float' and not the docks. Early in the 19th century William Jessop designed a new enclosed harbour to eradicate difficulties involved in loading and unloading vessels at the mercy of the River Avon's considerable tides. But Bristol's maritime tradition goes back much further than this, and many a fortune was acquired in the 'triangular trade': guns to Africa, slaves to America, sugar, rum, tobacco and cotton back. Coastal trade was also an important tradition. The quayside at Welsh Back, now reminiscent of Amsterdam in its cobbled, tree-lined

ambience, once reverberated to the clamour of Welsh voices whose owners had sailed over in trows with cargoes of slate and stone and coal. Beyond Bristol Bridge a defunct brewery was formerly a busy user of water transport as well, and the importing of sherry was another activity closely associated with the port of Bristol. Trade ceased in the Floating Harbour in the 1970s but it doesn't take too much imagination to picture the vibrant scenes of the past which characterised the

continued on page 6

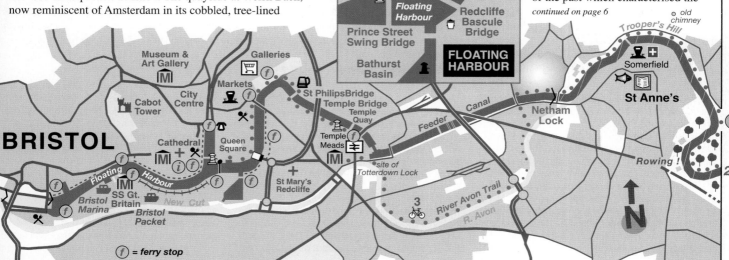

continued from page 5

Floating Harbour during the city's mercantile heyday.

In the absence of one's own boat it is still easy to explore the city centre by water courtesy of the frequent ferries which operate all the way from Temple Quay in the east (adjacent to Temple Meads railway station) to Cumberland Basin in the west (by the entrance lock to the tidal Avon). The best public moorings for visiting boaters are to be found on a pontoon just west of Prince Street Swing Bridge. They offer handy and rapid access to the city centre. Both Prince Street and the neighbouring Redcliffe Bascule Bridge have sufficient headroom for most inland waterway craft without needing to be swung or raised respectively.

Walkways more or less intact on either bank permit pedestrian exploration of the Floating Harbour, where the former Industrial Museum is in the process of being regenerated into a new Museum of Bristol, due to open in 2009 at the cost of a cool £18m. Railway tracks remain in situ creating an atmosphere of days gone by when much transhipment occurred. Sadly all the lines have been uprooted on the opposite side of the harbour where signs used to advise drivers to desist from shunting during periods when services were being held in the adjoining Cathedral.

How nice it would be to return to those days. In the mid Fifties something

in the region of ten thousand ships per annum were visiting the Port of Bristol, though the larger vessels involved used the docks at Portishead and Avonmouth as their tonnage precluded passage upstream through the restrictive Avon Gorge where the tidal range was close to fifty feet. The City Docks hosted the coastal and Continental trade, vessels up to a maximum of about fifteen hundred tons. Many traded from the Baltic and Scandinavia with timber and woodpulp for Bristol's paper-makers. From warmer climes came wine from Portugal, Spanish grapefruits and South African oranges.

Passing beneath the phalanx of railway tracks which form the northern approach to Temple Meads station, boaters make their way out of the city along the Feeder Canal as far as Netham Lock. This is not a particularly salubrious part of the city in terms of general appearance. Depending on tide levels, Netham Lock may well be open to pass through without operating. Beyond it steer well clear of the weir which takes the Avon downstream towards the open sea. Useful shopping facilities are available at St Anne's, though you may have to improvise when mooring and this is definitely not a spot for a lengthy stay.

Bristol (Map 1)

Hometown of such disparate characters as John Cabot, Isambard Kingdom Brunel and Cary Grant, Bristol is a terrific city, full of atmospheric passages and corners, alleyways and stairways as befits a former sea-trading port. Though much damage was brought about by bombing raids during the Second World War, a sense of unity has been restored and the melding of old and new has been more successful here than in say Plymouth or Coventry for instance. Two magnificent churches cry out for your attention, the Cathedral and St Mary's, Redcliffe. Elizabeth I described the latter as the fairest church in England.

Eating & Drinking

BORDEAUX QUAY - Pero's Bridge. Tel: 0117 943 1200. Former dockside wine warehouse revitalised as a brasserie, restaurant, bar and deli with the emphasis on regionally sourced foods. BRIDGE INN - Passage Street. *Good Beer Guide* recommended Bath Ales pub adjacent to St Philips Bridge and convenient for Temple Quay. Lunches but no food in the evenings. GLASS BOAT - Welsh Back. Tel: 0117 929 0704. Floating restaurant of considerable appeal by Bristol Bridge. Breakfasts, lunches, dinners. LOCKSIDE - Cumberland Basin. Tel: 0117 925 5800. Ubiquitous cafe/restaurant open from 7am Mon-Fri (8am Sat) but only Thur-Sat evenings. Old fashioned values in a splendid setting. LLANDOGER TROW - King Street. Tel: 0870 7001342. Tourist-conscious confection of a 17th century inn named after a village on the Wye which regularly traded with Bristol, thought to be the 'Spyglass Inn' of Stevenson's *Treasure Island*. Greene King portfolio beers.

Shopping

Beat a path to ST NICHOLAS & CORN STREET MARKETS, reminiscent of Oxford's wonderful indoor market, you'll find them just north of Bristol Bridge. Farmers' Market every Wednesday. Slow Food Market on the first Sunday of every month.

These independent traders meet their antithesis in the nearby BROADMEAD shopping centre. CHRISTMAS STEPS & ST MICHAEL'S is an imaginative shopping quarter in the vicinity of Colston Street.

Things to Do

TOURIST INFORMATION - Harbourside. Tel: 0906 711 2191 *www.visitbristol.co.uk*
BRISTOL FERRY BOAT CO - Tel: 0117 927 3416. Commendably frequent services (including an all year round commuter operation supported by the city council) make the ferries an ideal way of seeing much of the city if you haven't brought your own boat with you.
CITY SIGHTSEEING - Tel: 0870 444 0654. Open top bus tours, a great way to get to know the city.
CLIFTON SUSPENSION BRIDGE VISITOR CENTRE - Sion Place. Tel: 0117 974 4664. Surprise, surprise, Brunel's wonderful bridge took thirty years from conception to completion, delayed by financial problems, social riots and indecision. Learn all this and more before going to see the bridge itself.
SS GREAT BRITAIN - Great Western Dockyard. Tel: 0117 929 1843. Brunel's first great ocean liner built in 1843. The museum also provides an occasional home to a working replica of John Cabot's *Matthew* in which he crossed the Atlantic and bumped into Newfoundland in 1497.
BRITISH EMPIRE & COMMONWEALTH MUSEUM - Temple Meads. Tel: 0117 925 4980. The rise and fall of the British Empire and its sphere of influence housed in Brunel's original Bristol railway station of 1840. Thoroughly recommended.
CITY MUSEUM & ART GALLERY - Queen's Road. Tel: 0117 922 3571.
@BRISTOL - Harbourside. Tel: 0845 345 1235.

Multi-disciplined, 'hands on' visitor centre of special appeal to families.

Connections

BUSES - Tel: 0845 6020 156.
TRAINS - Tel: 08457 484950. Useful local services via Keynsham to Bath and beyond.

Hanham   (Map 2)

OLD LOCK & WEIR - riverside. Tel: 0117 967 3793. Unspoilt pub featured in Conan Doyle's adventure *Micah Clark*. Moorings for patrons.
CHEQUERS - riverside. Tel: 0117 967 4242. So close to its neighbour (above) that there's really no excuse for not trying both. Slightly smarter perhaps. Customer moorings.

Keynsham   (Map 2)

Surely no child of the Sixties can ever think of Keynsham and not hear Horace Batchelor slowly ennunciating the way to spell it on Radio Luxembourg. Further nostalgia emanates from the chocolate factory, originally erected by Frys of 'Five Boys' bar fame. Do you remember their faces? : desperation, expectation, realisation, pacification and acclamation! In the 1920s the works employed almost five thousand and a model housing estate was built for them called Somerdale. Much automated, the workforce is down to around six hundred now and the factory trades under the all encompassing brand name of Cadbury's.

Eating & Drinking

LOCK KEEPER - by Keynsham Lock. Tel: 0117 986 2383. Cosy lockside pub offering Young's ales (a long way west of Wandsworth - or Bedford for that matter!) and food.

Shopping

Plenty of shops and banks etc in the town centre less than ten minutes walk from the Avon via the railway station.

Connections

TRAINS - Tel: 08457 484950. Useful local services to Bath and Bristol.

Saltford   (Map 3)

Snug village of quiet by-roads away from the A4. The Manor house is of Norman origin. Handel is said to have been rhythmically inspired by the hammers in Saltford Brass Mill.

Eating & Drinking

JOLLY SAILOR - by Saltford Lock. Tel: 01225 873002. Popular waterside inn offering a good range of food. Customer moorings.
BIRD IN HAND - High Street. Tel: 01225 873335. Well worth the stroll up from the river for a game of petanque in the garden overlooking the Bristol-Bath cycleway, but a convivial atmosphere inside and good food. Butcombe, Abbey ales etc.
THE RIVERSIDE - overlooking Kelston Lock. Tel: 01225 873862. Modern restaurant pub developed with adjacent marina. Wadworth beers and a wide range of food. Customer moorings.

Shopping

Useful (if not extensive) range of shops on A4 - chemist, Co-op, newsagent, post office etc.

Swineford   (Map 3)

Eating & Drinking

THE SWAN - Tel: 0117 932 3101. Nicely refurbished wayside inn featuring an impressive cast list of hand-pumped, locally-brewed Bath Ales. An excellent menu too.

SPRING tides occasionally lick their salty tongue up as far as Keynsham, but for the most part, other than after heavy rain, the Avon is pliant enough and the only boating hazards are the weirs which would draw the unwary away from the lock channels. In comparison to the Warwickshire Avon, this one is under-sung; mistakenly considered a mere prelude or coda to the Kennet & Avon Canal proper. Beese's Tea Garden has been a popular haunt since 1846 and can be reached by ferry at the weekends. Wild asparagus thrives in the neighbouring woodlands.

Scenically the landscape pivots on Hanham: to the east the valley is wide and watermeadowy; to the west wooded and gorge-like. Few buildings are foolhardy enough to encroach too closely upon the mercurial river, but here and there lies evidence of old industries which once needed to be near to the river because they relied upon it for transport: various light industries occupy premises - conspicuously dated 1881 - formerly used as a soap works; a weigh bridge office remains at Londonderry Wharf

where coal was once loaded on to barges; Hanham Colliery stood in what is now woodland on the north bank of the river downstream of the high A4174 road crossing; an old copper smelting chimney overlooks the river as it winds past the now domestic entrails of St Anne's Park where board mills and a tar distillery provided river trade up until the 1960s. Cadbury's chocolate factory at Keynsham dates from the 1920s but has the look of a Lancashire textile mill. On Keynsham Hams the beginning of the end for the Monmouth Rebellion took place in 1685 when the Duke of Beaufort's Cavalry routed the rebels prior to the bloody denouement at Sedgemoor. The imposing 17th century tower of Keynsham's parish church looms over the high embankment which carries the railway over the meadowlands. The Avon Valley Railway has breathed fresh life into the old Midland Railway line which linked Bath with Mangotsfield.

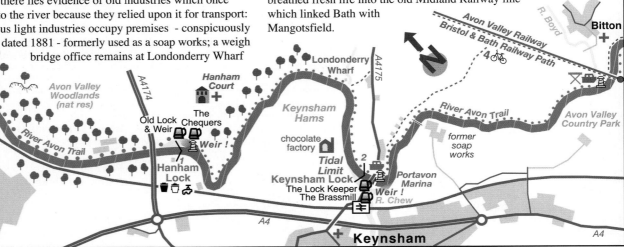

THE River Avon shares its journey between Bristol and Bath with the A4 trunk road, the Great Western main line, and the course of the old Midland Railway which has been reborn as the "Bristol & Bath Railway Path", one of the earliest Sustrans projects which have brought admirable new use to abandoned railways; though, nostalgically, one might be forgiven for day-dreaming that your boat might be overtaken at any moment by the Pines Express! Beyond the valley floor, however, your focus is apt to be drawn to the rolling hills which fill the northern horizon. With time on your hands, and having secured suitable moorings (something at a premium on the Avon)

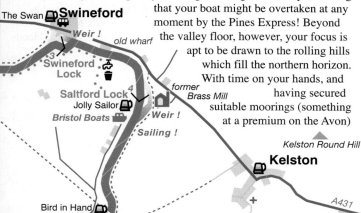

you might rewardingly essay a walk or two in this direction. Not that the river lacks inherent interest as it meanders from lock to lock, though one or two of its tighter bends have been ironed-out in recent times to lessen the threat of flooding.

One of the most potent images on this section of your journey is the ivy clad annealing ovens that are remnants of Kelston's former brass mill. They overlook the river by Saltford Lock and date from early in the 18th century when the mill employed the power of the Avon in the shaping of metal. There was also a brass mill at Swineford.

The mile long straight above Kelston Lock is used as a training reach by rowers- beware their wash! The grounds of Kelston Park were designed by Capability Brown.

The A4 elegantly crosses the river at New Bridge. The railway bridges have less aesthetic value, but at least they provide pedestrians with the opportunity to cross the river in the regrettable absence of former ferries. New Bridge was the western terminus of Bath's tramway system between 1904 and 1939. Three busy boatyards create considerable traffic on a stretch of inland waterway not readily associated with a high percentage of boating activity.

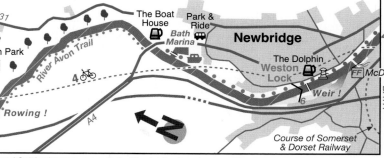

For details of facilities at Swineford and Saltford turn to page 7; for Newbridge turn to page 13

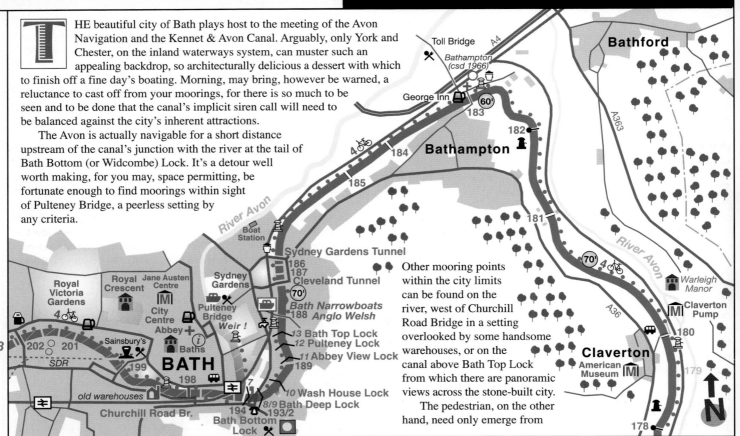

T HE beautiful city of Bath plays host to the meeting of the Avon Navigation and the Kennet & Avon Canal. Arguably, only York and Chester, on the inland waterways system, can muster such an appealing backdrop, so architecturally delicious a dessert with which to finish off a fine day's boating. Morning, may bring, however be warned, a reluctance to cast off from your moorings, for there is so much to be seen and to be done that the canal's implicit siren call will need to be balanced against the city's inherent attractions.

The Avon is actually navigable for a short distance upstream of the canal's junction with the river at the tail of Bath Bottom (or Widcombe) Lock. It's a detour well worth making, for you may, space permitting, be fortunate enough to find moorings within sight of Pulteney Bridge, a peerless setting by any criteria.

Other mooring points within the city limits can be found on the river, west of Churchill Road Bridge in a setting overlooked by some handsome warehouses, or on the canal above Bath Top Lock from which there are panoramic views across the stone-built city.

The pedestrian, on the other hand, need only emerge from

Map labels:

Bathford

Toll Bridge
Bathampton (csd 1966)
George Inn
60'
183
182
184
185
181
70'
Bathampton

River Avon

Boat Station
Sydney Gardens Tunnel
186
187
Cleveland Tunnel
70'
Bath Narrowboats
188 *Anglo Welsh*
13 Bath Top Lock
12 Pulteney Lock
11 Abbey View Lock
189
10 Wash House Lock
8/9 Bath Deep Lock
194
193/2
Bath Bottom Lock
7
198
199
202 201
SDR
old warehouses
Churchill Road Br.

Royal Victoria Gardens
Royal Crescent
Jane Austen Centre
City Centre
Sydney Gardens
Pulteney Bridge
Abbey
Weir !
Sainsbury's
Baths
BATH

Warleigh Manor
Claverton Pump
180
179
178
Claverton
American Museum

River Avon

A4   A363   A36

N

For details of facilities in Bath turn to pages 12 & 13

Bath Spa railway station (for no Pearson aficionado would be crass enough to come by car!) to find his or her way on to the towpath by way of Halfpenny Footbridge after which it's a simple heads or tails choice between exploring the river to the west or the canal to the east.

The River Avon

The River Avon plunges over Pulteney Weir before establishing its true navigable status. Trip boats, however, ply the picturesque reach above the weir upstream as far as Bathampton; whilst at Bath Boat Station, half a mile or so upstream, punts and skiffs may be hired for halcyon dalliances with one's current inamorata.

Other trip boats ply their trade downstream of Pulteney Weir as the river wends its way past Bath Rugby Club's well known Recreation Ground on one bank and the elegant Parade Gardens on the other. A substantial bridge carries North Parade Road over the river and then Isambard Kingdom Brunel's Great Western Railway spans the water before the site of Dolmead Wharf is reached beside the entrance to the canal. In the 18th century much of the stone used in the construction of Bath's classical thoroughfares came down by tramway to this point. A good deal of it was despatched along the Avon for export via Bristol to points as far afield as Dublin.

Halfpenny Footbridge tragically collapsed in 1877, overloaded by crowds on their way to the Bath & West Show, considerable loss of life ensued. The railway crosses the river a second time before Churchill Bridge is encountered, a rather bland modern replacement for Bath Old Bridge, an attractive three-arched structure of mid eighteenth century origin. The warehouses on the south bank which follow are a reminder of lost river trade. You may moor opposite (though railings, inexplicably, create something of an obstacle) and imagine you've arrived with a cargo of grain ex Avonmouth.

Around the next bend come memories of one of Britain's best loved railways, the incomparable Somerset & Dorset system, which ran out of Bath's Green Park station across the Mendip Hills to Bournemouth. This gracious terminus, whose booking hall might easily be mistaken for an elegant town house, witnessed its last trains depart in a flurry of steam in 1966, but has survived more or less intact to become part of an indoor market and a Sainsbury's supermarket - one does not know whether to smile or to cringe. Old photographs depicting the Pines Express storming up the 1 in 50 to Combe Down's suffocatingly confined tunnel, invariably expose a backdrop of gasholders which survive, incongruous now amidst retail parks and other 21st century paraphernalia. Gas tar was loaded on to barges for conveyance to Bristol until as comparatively recently as 1967. A suspension bridge - reminiscent in its less grandiloquent way of the one at Marlow on Map 34 - adds dignity and interest to the scene.

The Kennet & Avon Canal

Bath Bottom Lock is numbered 7th in the sequence from Bristol. Numbers 8 and 9 were combined when the canal was restored at this point in 1976. The new chamber has an intimidating depth of 19ft 5ins, those inclined to claustrophobia and/or vertigo are advised to watch proceedings from a safe distance. Succeeding locks ascend the hillside in an agreeable manner, several of them sport ornamented iron footbridges at their tails cast locally by Stothert & Pitt in their riverside foundry. Abbey View Lock fulfils its obligations and lock-wheelers may make the most of the view.

Bath Top Lock marks the beginning of a lengthy pound which would be half as much again longer were it not for the solitary lock at Bradford, ten miles away. A useful boatyard and hire base follows before the canal romantically skirts the periphery of Sydney Gardens, encountering two tunnels and two elegant iron footbridges dated 1800. Cleveland House Tunnel is 173 feet long and the towpath runs through it. Above stands Cleveland House, former headquarters of the Kennet & Avon Canal Company. A trap-door in the tunnel roof was employed for facilitating the exchange of paperwork between clerks above and bargees below.

Sydney Gardens were opened as a 'resort of pleasure' in 1795, they were provided with an hotel, a bowling green and a labyrinth. The canal builders had to pay handsomely to invade the gardens' serenity. Thirty years later that calm was disturbed again by the passage of the London to

Bristol railway. At 165 yards, Sydney Gardens Tunnel is slightly shorter than its neighbour. Emerging from its eastern portal the canal runs shelf-like above the Avon Valley, shaking off the suburbs and sensing open countryside. Bridge 185 is a footbridge which replaced a swingbridge called Folly after a nearby pub was destroyed during a Second World War bombing raid. The main London and Bristol railway line runs invisibly below, though passing trains break the silence, not, however, as intrusively as the relatively new stretch of A4 dual carriageway, confirmation that each new era of transport is more destructive than the last.

Essaying the easiest route around the hem of Bathampton Down, the canal continues to keep company with the River Avon, journeying on an almost north-south axis between Bathampton itself and Claverton. The scenery is delicious, and decidedly 'West Country' in feel, not something the canal network is necessarily well-acquainted with. A tramway was employed to bring stone down to Hampton Quarry Wharf by Bridge 182 when the canal was being built.

Claverton Pump was built to bring water up from the Avon to fill the canal. It was the work of John Rennie and its two water-wheels first began operating in 1813. It worked manfully for barely less than a century and a half before being replaced by a diesel pump. In 1976, however, it was lovingly restored by the Kennet & Avon Canal Trust. Whilst electric pumps do most of the work nowadays, the water-wheels perform their ancient rites on special days to an admiring public.

Bath   (Map 4)

One doesn't need Unesco's 'World Heritage Site' seal of approval to facilitate the savouring of Bath's cohesive loveliness. By any criteria, this is one of Europe's most beautiful cities, and since one hasn't been able for almost forty years to arrive by steam train at the Queen Square (latterly Green Park) terminus of the Midland Railway, the Kennet & Avon Canal offers a consolatory alternative for visitors whose senses are fine-tuned to the more lofty ramifications of travel. The Roman Baths illustrate how far Bath's civilisation goes back, but it was the 18th century Welshman Beau Nash who galvanised the city's fame as a watering hole with few rivals. As Master of Ceremonies, he was the Tourism Development Officer of his era, and his grasp of publicity brought Society's crowds flocking to Bath as much for the social scene as for the quality of the waters. If Nash was Bath's best publicist, the architects John Wood, father and son, were the men most responsible for the city's inherent beauty and there is no way you should leave before inspecting the extraordinary Royal Crescent, the Pump Room or Pulteney Bridge, let alone the 15th century Abbey and the Baths themselves. Make the most of it!

Eating & Drinking

GREEN PARK BRASSERIE - Tel: 01225 338565 www.greenparkbrasserie.com Stylish bistro type restaurant housed in former station building, eat heartily then catch the ghost train to Evercreech Junction or wait for the live jazz Wed-Sat evenings. Internet cafe. Butcombe bitter on tap.

HOP POLE - Upper Bristol Road. Tel: 01225 446327. Bath Ales pub easily accessed from towpath at Bridge 201. Great food, sublime beer.

FISHWORKS - Green Street. Tel: 01225 448707 www.fishworks.co.uk Fascinating combination of fishmonger, fish restaurant and cooking school - see also under Shopping.

OLD GREEN TREE - Green Street. Tel: 01225 448259. RCH from Somerset and Wickwar from Gloucestershire are regulars on tap in this wonderful time-warp of a pub. Lunches.

THE RAVEN - Queen Street. Tel: 01225 425045. Lively, refurbished real ale pub which features in the Good Beer Guide. Famed for its pies!

HANDS TEAROOM - Abbey Street. Tel: 01225 463928. Traditional tearoom, beautifully furnished.

SALLY LUNN'S - North Parade Passage. Tel: 01225 461634 www.sallylunns.co.uk A Bath institution which charmingly contrives to transcend its tourist status as the city's oldest house and the home of the world famous Bath Bun. Tea room and restaurant facilities.

IL TOCCO D'ITALIA - Spring Gardens Road. Tel: 01225 311184 www.iltocco.co.uk Contemporay Italian overlooking Pulteney Weir.

LE PETIT COCHON - Widcombe Parade. Tel: 01225 317204 www.lepetitcochon.co.uk Authentic French bistro easily reached to south of Bottom Lock.

BATHWICK BOATMAN - Bathwick. Tel: 01225 428844 www.bathwickboatman.com Elegant boathouse restaurant on the isolated yet navigable reach of the Avon between Pulteney Weir and Bathampton Weir. Build up an appetite by punting first!

THE DOLPHIN - waterside, Weston Cut. Tel: 01225 445048. All day family orientated pub, moorings adjacent - see Map 3.

THE BOATHOUSE - Newbridge Road. Tel: 01225 482584. Brains (of Cardiff) ales, plush interiors, extensive menu and waterside gardens with customer moorings - see Map 3.

Shopping

Avoid the city centre chain stores and you'll be well rewarded. The GUILDHALL MARKET is a good starting point, it's located between the High Street and Pulteney Bridge. GREEN PARK MARKET is housed in the gracious environment of the old Midland Railway terminus. Arts and crafts feature Wednesday to Saturday, and there is a Farmers' Market on Saturdays as well. It is feasible to moor nearby on the Avon and stock up the galley at SAINSBURY'S, but Bath's handsome thoroughfares are filled with independent retailers, and it's much more fun to seek out the likes of THE SAUSAGE SHOP and FISHWORKS on Green Street, WHITEMANS bookshop on Orange Grove and BAYNTUNS antiquarian bookshop and book-binding specialist on Manvers Street near the railway station.

Things To Do

TOURIST INFORMATION - Abbey Churchyard. Tel: 0906 711 2000 www.visitbath.co.uk

CITY SIGHTSEEING - open top bus tours of Bath and its environs. Office at the railway station. Tel: 01225 330444 www.city-sightseeing.com

THE ROMAN BATHS & PUMP ROOM - Abbey Churchyard. Tel: 01225 477785.

THERMAE BATH SPA - Hot Bath Street. Tel: 01225 331234 www.thermaebathspa.com Thermal baths and steam rooms including spectacular rooftop pool.

JANE AUSTEN CENTRE - Gay Street. Tel: 01225 443000 www.janeausten.co.uk Bath was the setting for Northanger Abbey and Persuasion and their authoress lived in the city from 1801 to 1806.

MUSEUM OF BATH AT WORK - Julian Road. Tel: 01225 318348. A fascinating antidote to Bath's (understandable) tendency to 18th century overkill.

WILLIAM HERSCHEL MUSEUM - New King Street. Tel: 01225 446865. Small museum in former home of famous astronomer.

NO.1 ROYAL CRESCENT - Tel: 01225 428126.

HOLBURNE MUSEUM - Tel: 01225 466669. Art gallery located by Sydney Gardens within easy reach of the canal before/after tackling all those locks.

BATH BOATING STATION - Forester Road. Tel: 01225 466407. Rowing boat and punt hire on the isolated reach of the Avon between Bath and Bathampton.

MUSEUM OF COSTUME - Assembly Rooms. Tel: 01225 477173. Fashion through the ages.

Connections

BUSES - Tel: 0870 608 2 608.

TRAINS - Tel: 08457 484950. Useful links with Bradford-on-Avon, Keynsham and Bristol for towpath walkers and cyclists.

TAXIS - Abbey Cars. Tel: 01225 444444.

Bathhampton   (Map 4)

Bathampton was, until 1983, the site of Harbutt's Plasticine factory, something that generations of children had been thankful for since William Harbutt invented the substance in 1897. The canalside church will be of interest to Australian boating parties for the first Governor of New South Wales lies buried here whilst the interior features a small Australian Chapel. There are views eastwards to Brown's Folly, a hillside tower constructed to provide employment following the Napoleonic Wars.

Eating & Drinking

THE GEORGE INN - canalside Bridge 183. Tel: 01225 425079. Country inn predating the canal and said to be haunted by the loser of the last legally fought duel in England.

OUT & OUT - riverside (down from Bridge 183). Tel: 01225 469758. All day family restaurant/pub.

Claverton   (Map 4)

CLAVERTON PUMPING STATION - canalside Bridge 180 (walk down Ferry Lane and over the railway level crossing. Tel: 01225 483001. Generally open April to October on Weds, Suns and Bank Holidays but only in operation on special pumping days - see local notices or telephone for further information. www.claverton.org On no account should this be missed if at all possible!

AMERICAN MUSEUM - Claverton Manor. Substantial early 19th century mansion housing fascinating displays of Americana. Tel: 01225 460503. Light refreshments available. Open Easter to October afternoons but not usually Mondays except during August and Bank Holidays www.americanmuseum.org

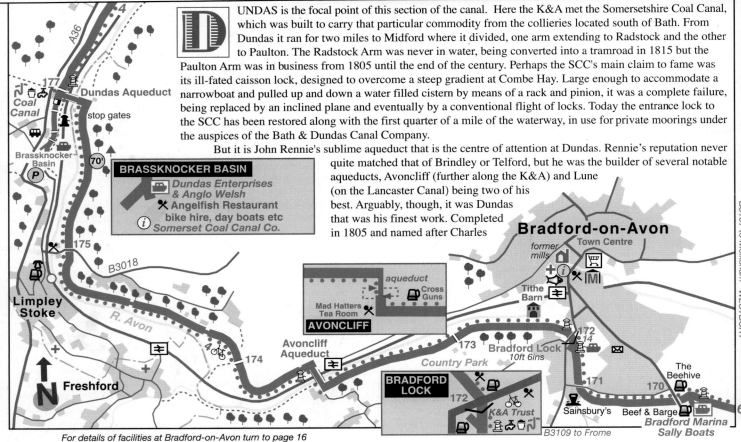

UNDAS is the focal point of this section of the canal. Here the K&A met the Somersetshire Coal Canal, which was built to carry that particular commodity from the collieries located south of Bath. From Dundas it ran for two miles to Midford where it divided, one arm extending to Radstock and the other to Paulton. The Radstock Arm was never in water, being converted into a tramroad in 1815 but the Paulton Arm was in business from 1805 until the end of the century. Perhaps the SCC's main claim to fame was its ill-fated caisson lock, designed to overcome a steep gradient at Combe Hay. Large enough to accommodate a narrowboat and pulled up and down a water filled cistern by means of a rack and pinion, it was a complete failure, being replaced by an inclined plane and eventually by a conventional flight of locks. Today the entrance lock to the SCC has been restored along with the first quarter of a mile of the waterway, in use for private moorings under the auspices of the Bath & Dundas Canal Company.

But it is John Rennie's sublime aqueduct that is the centre of attention at Dundas. Rennie's reputation never quite matched that of Brindley or Telford, but he was the builder of several notable aqueducts, Avoncliff (further along the K&A) and Lune (on the Lancaster Canal) being two of his best. Arguably, though, it was Dundas that was his finest work. Completed in 1805 and named after Charles

BRASSKNOCKER BASIN
Dundas Enterprises & Anglo Welsh
Angelfish Restaurant
bike hire, day boats etc
Somerset Coal Canal Co.

AVONCLIFF
aqueduct
Cross Guns
Mad Hatters Tea Room

BRADFORD LOCK
172
K&A Trust

Coal Canal
Dundas Aqueduct
stop gates
Brassknocker Basin
175
B3018
Limpley Stoke
R. Avon
Freshford
Avoncliff Aqueduct
174
173
Country Park
former mills
Bradford-on-Avon
Town Centre
Tithe Barn
Bradford Lock
10ft 6ins
172
171
170
The Beehive
Sainsbury's
Beef & Barge
Bradford Marina Sally Boats
B3109 to Frome
177
70'

Dundas, the first chairman of the Kennet & Avon Canal Company, the 150-yard, three-arched aqueduct was built of Bath stone in the Doric style with a solid parapet featuring balustrading at each end, and cornices projecting some four feet from the parapet on both faces.

Crossing into Wiltshire, the canal glides through the delectable Limpley Stoke Valley seemingly without a care in the world. It wasn't always so, for the length between Limpley Stoke Bridge and Avoncliff Aqueduct became known as the 'dry section', so prone was it to leakage and landslips. The canal bed now has a layer of hardcore on a porous membrane, which is itself covered by a layer of polythene sheeting and a final bed of reinforced concrete.

A small community - pub, station, tearoom and cluster of houses - has grown up around Avoncliff Aqueduct. Similar to Dundas just down the valley, Avoncliff is a three-arched Bath stone structure, although there is evidence of extensive brick repair work, particularly to the eastern facade. It also had a tramroad link to a local quarry, in this case the Upper Westwood

Reflections at Avoncliff

Quarry to the south of the canal.

Bradford-on-Avon was where it all began as far as the Kennet & Avon Canal was concerned, the first sod being cut just outside the Canal Tavern in 1794. Reflect on the past - an army of unfortunate, ill educated navvies toiling laboriously away with picks and shovels by day, then drinking and brawling by night whilst you enjoy present day Bradford, one of the most picturesque ports of call on the entire K&A. There were once two wharves in this thriving wool town. Upper Wharf is especially attractive with dry dock, wharfinger's house and pub, together with a K&A Canal Trust shop and cafe. Half a mile to the east, opposite Bradford Marina, the nineteenth century Beehive Inn stands close to the proposed junction with the intended Dorset & Somerset Canal, scheduled to run via Frome, Wincanton and Sturminster Newton to Shillingstone Okeford near Blandford Forum. What a fantastic canal the D&S would have been, but although the enabling Act received Royal Assent in March 1796, work on the main line never actually began due to financial difficulties.

Monkton Combe (Map 5)

BRASSKNOCKER BASIN - an imaginative modern development at the junction of the Somerset Coal Canal. Attractions include the Angelfish Restaurant (Tel: 01225 723483); Dundas Enterprises (Tel: 01225 722292) for day boat, canoe and cycle hire and the Somerset Coal Canal Company - see Boating Directory page 94. The Kennet & Avon Canal Trust operate boat trips from the basin aboard *Jubilee* - see page 95.

Limpley Stoke (Map 5)

Pretty riverside community a short walk downhill from Bridge 175. There's a pub called the Hop Pole (Tel: 01225 723134) and a Thai restaurant. Look out for the old railway station (now a private home). The Camerton branch ran from here until the early 1950s and the much loved Ealing comedy *The Titfield Thunderbolt* was filmed on the line after it had been officially closed and some scenes were shot at the Hop Pole.

Avoncliff (Map 5)

Many canal users will be tempted to linger awhile at Avoncliff and savour the setting. Whilst most eyes will be drawn to the aqueduct, spare a moment to look at the tiny railway station, almost as pretty and as cared for as if it were on some preserved steam line. Refreshments can be obtained at the popular Cross Guns Inn (Tel: 01225 862335) or the Mad Hatter Tearooms - Tel: 01225 868123.

Bradford-on-Avon (Map 5)

Teetering on the brink of its clifftop setting, mellow, medieval Bradford-on-Avon resembles a small version of Bath, and being smaller can be appreciated and assimilated all the more easily. Its architecture appears capable of absorbing sunlight and then emitting it like storage heaters. Amongst many outstanding buildings you'll come upon a Saxon church, a tithe barn and a 14th century bridge with a chapel on it. One of an exclusive club of five remaining in England, regular Canal Companion users will easily be able to run through the locations of the other four! Bradford's fortunes were built on wool and weaving and many of its buildings, both domestic and commercial, reflect the heyday of this lost industry; solely the relentless tide of road traffic being able to deflect from the town's inherent beauty.

Eating & Drinking

LOCK INN CAFE - canalside below Bradford Lock. Wonderful establishment offering food, canoe and bike hire and an infectious sense of humour. Tel: 01225 868068. *www.thelockinn.co.uk*
K&A TRUST TEA ROOM - canalside above Bradford Lock. Tel: 01225 864779. Refreshments and canalia.
CANAL TAVERN - canalside below Bradford Lock. Tel: 01225 867426. Wadworth ales and a wide range of food.
THE MAHARAJA - adjacent canal wharf. Indian tandoori restaurant/take-away. Tel: 01225 866424.
GEORGIAN LODGE - Bridge Street. Tel: 01225 862268. Hotel and restaurant adjacent the river open to non-residents for lunches, dinners and afternoon teas. Nice courtyard and garden.
THAI BARN - Bridge Street. Tel: 01225 866433.

BRIDGE TEA ROOM - Bridge Street. Tel: 01225 865537. Charmingly old-fashioned tea room across the street from Bradford's lovely bridge.

Shopping

The town centre is less than ten minutes walk down from the canal and there are heaps of nice old-fashioned shops. We found two good delis - MAPLES and the CHEESE BOARD - a branch of the REAL MEAT COMPANY who specialise in free range and organic produce, and a small bookshop called EX LIBRIS. More prosaically, there's a SAINSBURY'S supermarket by Bridge 171.

Things to Do

TOURIST INFORMATION - Silver Street (adjacent to Town Bridge). Tel: 01225 865797.

Connections

TRAINS - connections for Bath via Avoncliff and Westbury via Trowbridge. Tel: 08457 484950.
TAXIS - Ashley Cabs. Tel: 01225 868111.

Trowbridge (Map 6)

One suspects that few canal users make the effort to visit Trowbridge, the County Town of Wiltshire, upon which the cloying smell of Pork Farms & Bowyers food processing plant hangs like a wet blanket. On foot it's a bleak trudge which takes the best part of half an hour. Buses from Hilperton alleviate such discomforts, but in truth Bradford or Devizes are better deserving of your curiosity, though here and there amongst the mediocrity are many handsome buildings in local stone which deserve a better setting.

Eating & Drinking

KINGS ARMS - Hilperton near Bridge 166. Tel: 01225 755168. Food, families welcome.

Shopping

Full range of shops and banks in the town centre. Interesting indoor market. Lidl supermarket about ten minutes walk from Hilperton Wharf. The petrol station near Bridge 166 has a useful shop, post office counter and cash machine.

Things to Do

TOURIST INFORMATION - St Stephens Place. Tel: 01225 777054.
TROWBRIDGE MUSEUM - Court Street. Tel: 01225 751339 *www.trowbridgemuseum.co.uk*

Connections

TRAINS - to/from Bath via Bradford. Tel: 08457 484950.
TAXIS - D2D Cars. Tel: 0800 085 4474.

Semington (Map 6)

SOMERSET ARMS - 5 minutes walk south of Bridge 160. Tel: 01380 870067. Comfortable old coaching inn.

Seend Cleeve (Map 7)

THE BARGE INN - canalside Bridge 154. Tel: 01380 828230. Very popular waterside pub. Wadworth beer and a wide range of food.
BREWERY INN - 5 minutes south from Bridge 154. Unspoilt village local. Tel: 01380 828463.

Seend (Map 7)

Gracious village somewhat compromised by traffic on the A361. Post office stores and pub.

Sells Green (Map 7)

THREE MAGPIES - north of Bridge 149. Tel: 01380 828389. Wadworths, bar and restaurant meals.

THE Kennet & Avon Canal skirts the urban periphery of Trowbridge. An Act was passed in 1769 to build a branch into the town but construction didn't ensue. Two modest, yet elegant aqueducts transport the canal over the River Biss, a tributary of the Avon, and the Westbury-Bath railway line respectively. The single arched Biss Aqueduct, whilst never soaring to the same heights (literally or metaphorically) as Dundas and Avoncliff further west, is especially handsome. And then there are the remains - admittedly scant - of two wharves beside Hilperton Road Bridge, Marsh Wharf and Hilperton Wharf both being built to serve Trowbridge in the absence of that branch. To the north the Shredded Wheat factory at Staverton is a prominent landmark - when the poet Edward Thomas bicycled past it in 1913, sourcing copy for *In Pursuit of Spring*, the mill was operating under the auspices of the Phoenix Swiss Milk Company!

It's difficult to visualise sleepy Semington as a busy canal junction but such was the case in the early part of the 19th Century. The Wilts & Berks Canal, opened in 1810, ran from here for fifty heavily locked miles to the Thames at Abingdon (see Map 24) via Melksham, Swindon and Challow. Its commercial success was short-lived, however, competition from the GWR from London to Bristol bringing about its downfall. Through traffic became impossible following the collapse of an aqueduct between Chippenham and Calne in 1901. Little evidence of the junction remains, except for the toll collector's house, now in private ownership, the old stop lock being hidden under the obviously keen gardener's immaculate collection of sweet peas, lavender and hollyhocks. The Wilts & Berks Canal Trust are ambitiously campaigning to restore the canal to full navigation and have the support of a number of local authorities. A number of sections have already been returned to water, but full re-opening will be a both costly and time consuming project. The two locks at Semington mark the end of a five mile level pound from Bradford-on-Avon, and they are quickly followed by a flight of five at Seend. A new aqueduct carries the canal across the new A350.

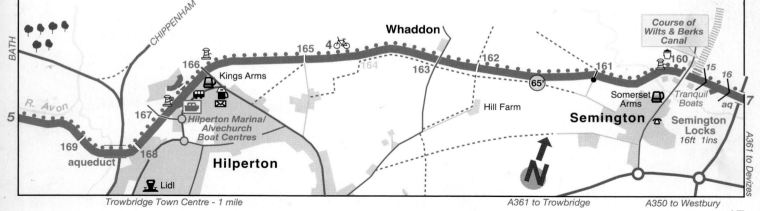

HOW green and lush is the countryside around Seend Cleeve. Swing bridges abound, and there's a flight of five locks too, giving you extra time to appreciate the soft rolling hills that characterise this part of Wiltshire. The Barge Inn, situated below the middle lock of the flight, is one of the most popular pubs on the entire K&A and stands on the site of Seend Wharf. Dating back to 1805, The Barge comprises the former wharf house and stables and was once owned by the Duke of Somerset's family. In 1916 it became the home of the 'Wiltshire Giant' Fred Kempster (8 feet 2 inches) whose brother-in-law was the landlord.

A field to the east of The Barge was the site of a most unlikely industry in the nineteenth century, ironstone having been discovered on Seend Hill. Two blast furnaces were built, together with tramway connections to the canal and a branch railway to Devizes, but the enterprise was never a financial success. Nevertheless, mining of iron ore continued until after the First World War. The lines of the two tramways are still discernible, whilst the elaborate house of the iron master is visible on the hillside above the canal.

Distant views of Salisbury Plain, some twenty miles away to the south, present themselves as the canal drifts across Summerham Brook on a small aqueduct. Ever mindful of maximising water supply, the K&A utilises water from the brook which is channelled into the waterway via the Seend Feeder.

Lots of people seem to like mooring overnight between bridges 149 and 152. The countryside is blissful and paths radiate from the swing-bridges for the exercising of dogs. In doing so one might come upon the melancholy trackbed of an old railway which once linked Devizes with the outside world. Later, as the light fades, the campanologists of Seend may lull you to sleep.

Bridge 148 marks the site of Wragg's Wharf from which a family of that name once plied with a pair of boats to and from Dunkerton Colliery on the Somerset Coal Canal. Commercial trade on the Kennet & Avon petered out under Great Western Railway ownership, not surprisingly the railway company promoted trains at the expense of boats and by and large the local economies were happy to comply.

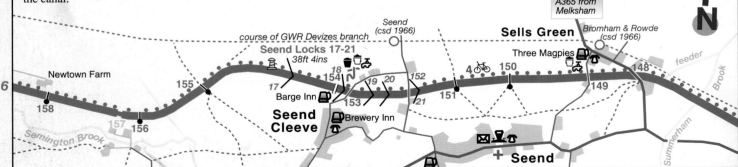

For details of facilities at Seend Cleeve, Seend and Sells Green turn back to page 16

Caen Hill Swans

DEVIZES Locks were the last major engineering works to be completed before the canal's opening in 1810, and one of the final restoration projects to be finished prior to reopening in 1990. The locks exert a powerful influence on the waterway to this day, with cruising itineraries being carefully planned around their intimidating presence.

But first some facts and figures. One of the 'Seven Wonders of the Waterways' as selected by Robert Aickman, the Devizes flight of 29 widebeam locks raises (or lowers) the level of the canal by 237 feet in just over two miles. They come in three groups: seven at Foxhangers, sixteen at Caen Hill and six at the town end of the flight. Whilst the locks were under construction in the early 1800s a tramroad provided a link between Foxhangers and Devizes, as evidenced by the towpath arches in the road bridges that cross the canal. The locks were built of brick, supplied by the now disused brickworks beside the Caen Hill section. To address serious water supply problems, a back pumping station was installed at Foxhangers in 1996, capable of returning 32 million litres of water per day to the top of the flight - equivalent to one lockful every eleven minutes.

Impressive though the entire Devizes flight may be, it is the Caen Hill section that wins all the plaudits - and deservedly so. It has been claimed that they are named after the home town of a group of French prisoners of war who were made to work here during the construction of the flight, but authoritative local sources insist that 'Canehill' was a 17th century name for the locality. The sixteen closely spaced Caen Hill locks make light work of a 1 in 30 gradient. Each lock is equipped with an extensive side pond, virtually a small reservoir, designed by John Rennie to guarantee an adequate water supply.

But how does it feel to arrive at the foot (or top) of the flight with all those locks ahead of you? Well you certainly won't be doing much else that day, five to six hours being considered a good performance for clearance of the flight. But don't be intimidated, for the locks are well maintained and relatively easy to operate, and, in high season at least, you'll probably have other boaters to share the work with you. Settle in to a rhythm, relax and enjoy every moment of one of the best experiences the waterway system has to offer. The surroundings

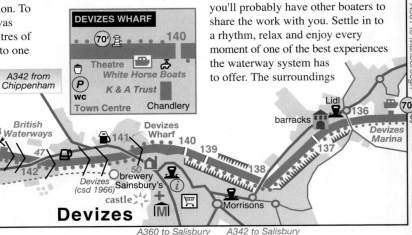

add to your enjoyment, being pleasantly pastoral with splendid views down the flight to the Avon Valley.

Devizes once possessed three wharves, Sussex, Lower and Town, of which only the latter survives. Built around 1812, its early trade was in coal from the Somersetshire Coal Canal, later traffic bringing in agricultural goods, brick, stone and timber; plus, of course, raw materials and finished products heading to and from Wadworth's brewery, situated less than a yard of ale's distance from the canal. Today two admirably restored buildings stand proudly on the wharf: a former warehouse now serves as the Wharf Theatre, whilst an erstwhile granary and wine store is now the headquarters of the Kennet & Avon Canal Trust. With a small hire fleet and trip boat also based here, the wharf buzzes with activity on summer weekends and is an excellent place to recuperate from (or gird your loins for) the rigours of the Devizes Locks.

Devizes (Map 8)

The Kennet & Avon is more fortunate than most canals when one considers the appeal of the towns it serves. Devizes is no exception - some might argue the best of them all. An ancient Wiltshire market town, it is widely known in beer-drinking circles for the excellence of the ale brewed by Wadworth, from whose lofty red brick premises a horse and dray still makes local deliveries about the town. David Verey's 1956 *Shell Guide to Wiltshire* spoke enthusiastically of the 'restrained dignity of its streets, the red brick Georgian houses contrasting with ashlar-faced public buildings in the Bath manner and the fine proportions of its market place' and half a century has failed to invalidate his opinion.

Eating & Drinking

CAEN HILL CAFE - canalside by Lock 44. Tel: 01380 724880. British Waterways information point and cafe for soups, sandwiches and home made cakes.
BLACK HORSE - Bath Road (by Bridge 142/Lock 47). Tel: 01380 723930. Wadworth pub with large canalside garden and a wide choice of food.
BEAR HOTEL - Market Place. Tel: 01380 722444. Reassuringly traditional old school hotel dating from 1599 offering morning coffees, bar lunches, afternoon teas, and evening meals. All Wadworth's heavenly ales on tap - and delivered, to boot, by horse and dray!
HEALTHY LIFE BISTRO - Little Brittox. Tel: 01380 720043. Part of TV chef Peter Vaughan's mini empire (see also under Shopping). Cafe Tue-Sat, 10am-3pm; evening bistro meals Tue-Sat from 7pm. Emphasis on natural and organic ingedients. *Fish & chips from Lees on Monday Market Street!*

Shopping

Shopping is fun in Devizes. Access from the Wharf is via Couch Lane and Snuff Street, beyond which the Market Place opens up in all its glory: Thursday is the main Market Day but there is also a Farmers' Market on the first Saturday in the month. Individual retail highlights include: the CONTINENTAL DELICATESSEN on High Street; the HEALTHY LIFE Natural Food Store on Little Brittox; GIDDINGS wine merchants on St John's Street and D'ARCY's secondhand bookshop on The Chequers. The COVERED MARKET is a lovely building in its own right: on Tuesdays it plays host to an antiques market, whilst on Thursdays, Fridays and Saturdays commerce is of a more general nature. Sainsbury's, Somerfield and Morrisons fight it out for your day to day needs.
WHARFSIDE CHANDLERY - Tel: 01380 725007.

Things to Do

DEVIZES VISITOR CENTRE - Market Place. Tel: 01380 729408. Tourist Information Centre plus displays delving into the town's colourful medieval heyday.
CANAL TRUST CENTRE - Devizes Wharf. Tel: 01380 729489. Excellent shop and museum operated by the Kennet & Avon Canal Trust.
WILTSHIRE HERITAGE MUSEUM - Long Street. Tel: 01380 727369. Rewarding museum, gallery and library owned by the Wiltshire Archaeological and Natural History Society.
WADWORTH SHIRES - Northgate. Open Monday to Friday 13.30 to 15.30. Wadworth's keep four Shire horses to make deliveries within a two mile radius of the town. Two horses haul each dray and each dray can carry up to three tons of beer.

Connections

BUSES - Devizes' train services were Beechinged irrevocably into a siding in 1966, so now one must rely on buses. The main routes lead to railheads at Trowbridge, Chippenham, Salisbury and Swindon; this latter via Avebury offering an excursion to see the Stones - Tel: 0870 608 2 608. The estimable Wigglybus provides access along the K&A corridor - Tel: 01249 460600.
TAXIS - Aces Taxis. Tel: 01380 729629.

SCUDDING clouds cast energetic shadows on the sculptured downs as the canal's dreamlike and curvaceous traverse of the Vale of Pewsey is punctuated by remote villages, for the most part now bereft of shops and pubs. The widespread use of brick surprises, outnumbering stone and thatch until you see pockets of chalk exposed on the downs and realise that it would not be an ideal building material.

Only the most time-constrained canal traveller will be able to resist a detour up on to the tumuli littered top of the downs, scaling the chalky escarpment to where the Wansdyke once delineated prehistoric territories. These Marlborough Downs form the highest part of Wiltshire, just falling short of a thousand feet above sea level. On a clear day, the locals say, you can see the spire of Salisbury Cathedral peeping out above its own plain to the south.

Hereabouts are the headwaters of another River Avon, not to be confused with the one in the title of the Kennet & Avon Canal. This Avon flows south off these chalky uplands, receives encouragement from the Wylye, the Nadder and the Bourne, and eventually reaches its inevitable appointment with the English Channel at Christchurch in Dorset.

This is the Long Pound, and it lives up to its name, consisting of fifteen restful, lock-less miles with only the odd swing bridge to disturb a boater's reverie. Time, perhaps, to picture yourself the captain of a widebeam, horse-drawn barge, Pewsey bound with grain from Bristol docks.

A361 from Swindon

A361 from Devizes

Bishops Cannings

133

132

Allington

70'

134

Horton

Bridge Inn

The Knoll
530ft

131

129

128

127

135

65'

130

10

N

Little Horton

All Cannings

Kings Arms

By-road to Etchilhampton

For details of facilities at Horton, Bishops Cannings and All Cannings turn to page 25

THE Alton Barnes White Horse is readily visible from the canal to the north in the vicinity of Honey Street. It was cut in 1812, though not without some delay after the original contractor decamped with the money. This part of Wiltshire is well known for its Crop Circles some of the most mysterious appearances of these strange configurations have occured in the vicinity of Alton Barnes. Moor hereabouts on a summer night and you may well see knots of crop circle enthusiasts huddled on the chalk hillsides anticipating signs of 'activity'!

Overlooked by a high, red brick chimney, Honey Street Wharf was owned by Robbins, Lane & Pinniger, the last regular commercial users of the canal between Avonmouth and Hungerford. Their barge *Unity* carried softwood from Avonmouth and timber from Hungerford to the Honey Street Wharf sawmill. The company also built many of the boats used on the K&A, Basingstoke Canal and River Wey prior to leaving the site in the late 1940s. Nowadays a timber yard and agricultural merchant provide Honey Street with at least some semblance of commercial activity. With tourist eyes we may object to such environmental

intrusion, but at least it reminds us why the canal was built.

Most imposing is the Barge Inn, not to be confused for a rendezvous with the one at Seend (Map 7). In earlier times it played an even more significant role in the life of Honey Street Wharf, being an important stabling point for boat horses, a bakery, a brewery and a slaughterhouse all rolled into one. Following a destructive fire in 1858, it was completely rebuilt within six months, testimony to its importance to canal trade and commerce. In recent years it has become a gathering point for 'croppies' anxious to learn the latest news! Near Bridge 123 there's a memorial to two airmen killed when their Albemarle bomber crashed hereabout in 1944.

The hills close in - Woodborough and Picked being less than half a mile from the canal - as you drift languidly past Wilcot, well known for its 'Wide Water' and its 'Ladies Bridge'. In an echo of events at Tixall Wide on the Trent & Mersey Canal, the K&A engineers collided with the intransigence of Lady Susannah Wroughton, who insisted that the canal cut through her grounds had to be in the guise of an ornamental lake. Ladies Bridge at the western end of the Wide was a similar gesture of appeasement to the gentility, the bridge being decorated with ornamental stonework and equipped with balustraded parapets.

Alton Barnes

Stanton St Bernard

Gibson's Boat Services

126

125

The Barge

124 Country Store

123

70'

Honey Street

122

Picked Hill
662ft

120

Wide Water

119

Wilcot

117

Golden Swan

116

11

By-road to Pewsey

9

N

By-road to Woodborough   *For details of facilities in Honey Street and Wilcot turn to page 25*

FIRMLY ensconced in the Vale of Pewsey, the canal skirts the lush grounds of Stowell Park complete with its classical mansion. Elegant Stowell Park Suspension Bridge, carrying a private footpath into the park, is of unusual construction, being made from jointed iron bars instead of the more usual platform hung on wire cable.

A deep tree lined cutting leads on to Pewsey Wharf. The village - as it appears to prefer to think of itself, even though it has the facilities of a small town - lies half a mile away down the A345, but the canal wharf attracts a goodly number of land-based visitors and pay & display car parking facilities are provided. Overlooked by 900 foot Martinsell Hill, the canal wends its lockless way through the Vale of Pewsey, undisturbed in its peaceful slumbers. However, if you're eastbound, prepare to make the acquaintance of the main London-Plymouth railway line, which comes close alongside hereabouts and is to become your almost constant companion for the remainder of the journey to Reading.

The Great Western Railway was unkind to the Kennet & Avon Canal. It bought it out in 1852 and allowed it to languish, though theoretically it remained open to navigation until Nationalisation in 1948, following which the British Transport Commission proposed its abandonment. Yet how compatible are rail and canal routes, how unobtrusively both blend into and complement the surrounding countryside - contrast the six-lane monstrosity that is the M4, not more than twenty miles away to the north. For us there is nothing more reassuring than mooring close by a railway, passing trains providing a comforting backdrop, not least in the wee small hours of the morning when man's sense of insecurity reaches its zenith. Speaking of zeniths, the K&A reaches its own summit at Wootton Rivers, where a flight of four locks raises the level by 32 feet to the heady heights of 450 feet above sea level. Having fallen into a state of disrepair in the Fifties, the locks were reopened in June 1973.

A345 from Marlborough

French Horn · Pewsey Wharf · 114 · 113 · school · Boatman's Rest · The Waterfront · A345 · Pewsey · 10 · 115 · 70' · P

Broomsgrove Farm · 112 · 70' · 111 · New Mill · Milkhouse Water · Littleworth

Wootton Rivers · 107 · 108 · 109 · 110 · 70' · 51 · 52 · Cuckoo's Knob

Lock 51 - Wootton Rivers Bottom *8ft 0ins*
Lock 52 - Heathy Close *8ft 1ins*

Horton   (Map 9)

BRIDGE INN - canalside Bridge 134. Tel: 01380 860273. Convivial Wadworth pub offering food and good moorings for an overnight stop.

Bishop Cannings   (Map 9)

Home of the original Moonrakers who claimed that they were idiotically attempting to rake the moon (for its cheese) from a pond when ambushed by an Exciseman who (rightly) suspected them of retrieving smuggled brandy from a pond. The explanation is said to have worked! There is a Wadworth pub called the CROWN INN - Tel: 01380 860218.

All Cannings   (Map 9)

A peaceful village with a strong community spirit which has resulted in re-opening of the village shop (Tel: 01380 862913) where, in addition to basic requisites, local produce is on sale. The KINGS ARMS is good as well - Tel: 01380 860328 and the Wiltshire Wigglybus which will pick you up to order by telephoning 01249 460600 and whisk you away to the fleshpots of Devizes and or Pewsey.

Wilcot   (Map 10)

Lots of thatched properties in evidence, grouped about a sizeable green curiously sporting just one set of goalposts. The GOLDEN SWAN is a nice Wadworth pub - Tel: 01672 562289. Food and accommodation.

Honey Street   (Map 10)

THE BARGE INN - canalside. Tel: 01672 851705. Atmospheric and historic canal pub offering a wide selection of food; a popular gathering point for crop-circle investigators.

Pewsey   (Map 11)

Focus of its fecund vale, Pewsey admirably repays the trouble taken to walk down from the wharf, though those less energetically predisposed can call from the wharf for a taxi or the Wigglybus. Personally, we feel that after a long stint at the tiller, the walk can only be good for you. Passing under the railway (whose station boasts copies of *Country Life* in the waiting room) one comes at length to Marshall's Bakery, the first welcome outlier of civilisation. A weatherbeaten statue depicting King Alfred (but erected to show local approval of the crowning of King George V) marks the right-angled commencement of High Street which crosses a pretty stream with a sandy bed, no less than the 'Hampshire' Avon.

Eating & Drinking

BOATMAN'S REST - Pewsey Wharf. Tel: 01672 564700. Cosy licenced cafe which will do you anything from a bacon bap to a steak. THE WATERFRONT - Pewsey Wharf. Tel: 01672 564020. Local ales from the Three Castles Brewery upstairs in former wharf building. THE FRENCH HORN - adjacent Bridge 114. Tel: 01672 562443. Charming brick built pub just north of the wharf, said to have gained its name from the use of a horn to summon French prisoners of war at work on the canal. The sophisticated menu includes wild boar and the beer is Wadworth. CHEQUERS BISTRO - High Street. Tel: 01672 564004. Family run daytime bistro where the food is freshly cooked to something approaching perfection. Opens 8.30am Mon-Sat and the bacon & eggs will set you up for the walk back to the boat.
Pewsey also boasts several fast food outlets.

Shopping

Pewsey is presided over by a sizeable Co-op supermarket but we made a bee-line for THOMSON'S excellent delicatessen on River Street - Tel: 01672 563323. There's a Lloyds TSB bank (with cash machine), newsagent and pharmacy. Small market on Tuesdays and Farmers' Market on the 2nd Thursday monthly.

Things to Do

HERITAGE CENTRE - Tel: 01672 562617. Delightful collection of local history housed in Whatley & Hiscock's former agricultural engineering works. open Apr-Oct, Mon-Fri and Sat (am only). Admission is gratis but donations are welcomed and thoroughly deserved.

Connections

BUSES - regular services run to Swindon and Salisbury; the latter worthy of an excursion perhaps. Tel: 0870 608 2 608. The Wigglybus will aid towpath instalments - Tel: 01249 460600. TRAINS - First Great Western services to/from Hungerford, Newbury, Reading and London Paddington with connections at Westbury for Trowbridge, Bradford and Bath. Tel: 08457 484950. TAXIS - Kennet Taxis. Tel: 01380 723129.

Wootton Rivers   (Map 11)

Idyllic canalside village with a most curious clock in its church and an excellent inn called the ROYAL OAK (Tel: 01672 810332) delightfully constructed of weatherboarding and thatch. Wadworth beers and guest ales. Free range eggs and home made preserves for sale by Lock 51. Sporadic buses to Marlborough, Pewsey and Great Bedwyn.

SOMEONE ought to write a book about canal summits: their generic traits, their inherent variety. Not only did the 18th century engineers have to climb, when they got to the top they had to find water. The Kennet & Avon's two mile summit does not present too many opportunities for water storage and is obviously hardly long enough to act as a linear reservoir. The solution came from Wilton Water, a small reservoir fed by springs, and a pair of pumping engines were provided to feed the summit. Two centuries later, little has changed other than provision of new electric pumps and preservation of the old steam monsters who originally did the work, more of which in a moment.

Meanwhile consider the summit itself. Burbage Wharf was built in the nineteenth century to handle trade from Marlborough, which never received its promised branch canal. The wharf's present wooden crane (itself now showing signs of age and scaffolded) is a replica of the original

which stood there until 1972; in its heyday it handled copious quantities of timber, stone, coal and agricultural produce. Adjacent Burbage Bridge, carrying the busy A338 Marlborough-Andover road, is an early example of a skew bridge, ie one that crosses the canal at an angle rather than at ninety degrees. John Rennie is thought to have been the first canal engineer to master the skew technique and further K&A examples include Beech Grove Bridge (No 98) at Crofton and Mill Bridge (No 97) at Great Bedwyn. The railway also had a goods facility at Burbage which had originally been conceived as an interchange point between the two transport modes. Once, however, the railway had provided a branch line to Marlborough use of the siding settled down to spasmodic cattle trains run in connection with Marlborough's cattle fairs. There were *two* railway lines linking Savernake (pronounced Saver*nack*) with Marlborough, a Great Western branch which terminated in the town and the Midland & South Western Railway, which linked Southampton with Cheltenham.

Skirting the periphery of Savernake Forest - 2,300 acres of mixed woodland criss-crossed by a network of paths - the canal dives headlong into Bruce Tunnel, named after Thomas Bruce, the Earl of Ailesbury, who owned

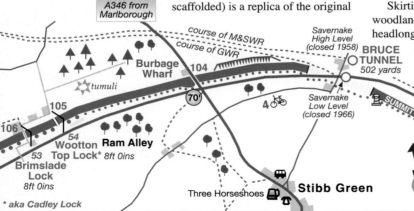

much of the land in the vicinity. It was perhaps ironic that the Kennet & Avon Canal Company should name the tunnel thus, for it was only on the good Earl's insistence that it had to be built at all. A deep cutting - like those on either side - would doubtless have coped with the low hill standing in the canal's way. At 502 yards long and wide enough for two narrowboats to pass inside, it's the only one worthy of the name on the entire K&A, and has no towpath, working boatmen pulling their craft through by chains fixed to the wall whilst their horses crossed above. Pedestrians still use the old horse path, of course, and, as is so often the case, are treated to much that the boater misses. The former Savernake Forest Hotel for example, and the remains of the two railway stations, and walkers alone can witness the railway's sleight of hand in crossing to the opposite bank of the canal while it passes unknowingly through its tunnel. Incidentally, the famous Gresley record-holder, *Mallard*, had to be ignominiously shunted into a siding at Savernake Low Level in 1948 after developing a defect whilst taking part in the Locomotive Exchanges which marked the beginning of the nationalised railway era.

All too quickly, the summit level is done with. Observe the feeder channel from Wilton Water and the remains of the bridge carrying the lines of the Midland & South Western Junction Railway across the canal as you approach the Crofton flight. Here nine locks drop you down by some sixty feet amidst the gently rolling hills that have become the canal's trademark. Crofton Pumping Station is famous enough to require little introduction, being one of the Kennet & Avon's 'must see' highlights. Initial proposals were for a lower and longer (eighteen-mile) summit level with a 4,300 yard tunnel extending almost to Wootton Rivers, but these were amended on the advice of William Jessop, which was readily accepted by John Rennie; hence the need for pumps to raise water from Wilton Water up forty feet to the higher summit. Two steam engines manfully did the job until 1959 when the removal of the top twenty feet of the pumphouse chimney resulted in insufficient draught for the boilers and they were replaced by first a diesel pump and then an electric one. The Crofton Society subsequently restored the steam pumps and the building, which was officially reopened by Sir John Betjeman in August 1970.

Stibb Green (Map 12)

Outlying part of Burbage approximately half a mile's walk from Bruce Tunnel. Bus connections to Marlborough (Tel: 0870 608 2 608) and a nice pub called the THREE HORSESHOES - Tel: 01672 810324 - which comes recommended by the illustrious *Good Beer Guide* for its Wadworth ales, home made food and railway memorabilia.

Savernake Forest (Map 12)

Savernake was a royal hunting forest and is mentioned in the Doomsday Book. The Grand Avenue of beech trees was planted by Capability Brown two hundred and fifty years ago. Less than a mile north of the canal stands the Ailesbury Column erected to give thanks for the recovery of George III from madness.

Crofton (Map 12)

Crofton Pumping Station houses two Cornish beam engines, the oldest built by Boulton & Watt dating from 1812, its junior a Harvey's of Hayle engine of 1845. Steam is raised through a hand-stoked, coal fired Lancashire boiler. Between them, the two engines can lift two tons of water to the summit at every stroke. Wilton Water was enlarged into a reservoir in 1836 and has become rich in birdlife. The pumping station is open to the public daily from Easter to the beginning of October, whilst the machinery itself comes to life on selected weekends - Tel: 01672 870300 for further information. An old Roman Road makes up part of a charming circular walk of just over an hour's duration based on Crofton. The Venta

Belgarum once linked Winchester with Mildenhall near Marlborough, now it will take you from the canal to Wilton Windmill which operates on Sunday and Bank Holiday Monday afternoons between Easter and the end of September - Tel: 01672 870427. Freshly milled flour is on sale and refreshments are available. Ironically, the mill had to be built in 1821 because the canal was taking too much water out of the River Bedwyn for local water mills to be driven. The windmill remained in everyday use until 1920. Restoration commenced in 1976. Nowadays it is floodlit from dusk until 10pm. For the sake of variety you can return along a footpath bordering Wilton Water, suitably refreshed, perhaps, following a visit to The Swan pub in Wilton village.

THIS is a classic section of the Kennet & Avon, much frequented by photographers and artists anxious to capture images of the canal in its parallel proximity to the Great Western main line. You might argue that the railway's cast list lacks variety nowadays - it would have been nice to have been here when 'Kings' were still entrusted to the *Cornish Rivieria Express* (or even 'Westerns' or 'Warships') - but there is still a thrill to be experienced as the canal traveller is overtaken by one of the ubiquitous High Speed Trains or, better still, by one of the lengthy stone trains.

The Battle of Bedwyn was fought here in 675 between Escuin, a Wessex nobleman who had seized the throne of Queen Saxburga, and the redoubtable King Wulfhere of Mercia. The fighting was fierce and the loss of life substantial before Escuin forced King Wulfhere to retreat northwards. The battle to restore this section of the Kennet & Avon Canal was far less bloody and ended with all the locks between Crofton and Hungerford being reopened by 1988.

Great Bedwyn Wharf, home to a small boatyard and base for a charitable trip boat, is unusual in that it was built on the towpath side. Whilst never handling as much trade as Burbage Wharf, three miles to the west, it once accommodated two coal merchants and was still shipping wheat to Aldermaston until just before the First World War.

Burnt Mill Lock was originally called Knight's Mill Lock, gaining its new name after Great Bedwyn water mill was destroyed by fire early in the 19th century. Two hundred years on, one mischievously wonders if it was 'an insurance job' following the reduction in flow associated with the advent of the canal. However, the infant River Dun certainly adds to the scene as the canal proceeds past Little Bedwyn which is where all the photographers like to gather. If they are out in numbers, their presence may well indicate the imminent appearance of a steam-hauled special.

The lazy, lockless miles of the Long Pound are but a distant memory now as the locks come along thick and fast. But there's a delightful timelessness about this little known corner of East Wiltshire that puts you in no mood to hurry.

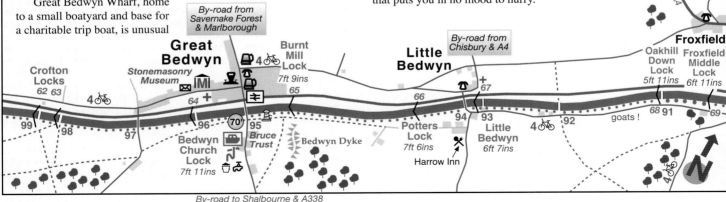

By-road from Savernake Forest & Marlborough

Great Bedwyn
Stonemasonry Museum

Crofton Locks
62 63

Burnt Mill Lock
7ft 9ins
65

By-road from Chisbury & A4

Little Bedwyn

Froxfield
Oakhill Down Lock
5ft 11ins

Froxfield Middle Lock
6ft 11ins

64

12

99
98
97
96
70'
95

Bedwyn Church Lock
7ft 11ins

Bruce Trust

Bedwyn Dyke

Potters Lock
7ft 6ins

Harrow Inn

94
93

Little Bedwyn
6ft 7ins

92

goats!

68 91
69

14

By-road to Shalbourne & A338

Great Bedwyn (Map 13)

The name Bedwyn is believed to have derived from 'Bedwind' or 'Bedwine', an old English word referring to a place where clematis grows in great profusion. One senses Great Bedwyn was a more important place in the past, at one time it returned two Members of Parliament! Nowadays it lies at the western edge of London's commuter belt - First Great Western's outer suburban service terminates here!

Eating & Drinking

CROSS KEYS - village centre. Tel: 01672 870678. Well appointed pub offering fresh food from locally sourced ingredients.
THREE TUNS - village centre. Tel: 01672 870280.

Shopping

Village stores open daily 7am-8pm except for Sundays when it closes at 1pm. The Post Office adjoins Lloyds stonemasonry workshop (Tel: 01672 870234) which features an astonishing collection of monuments. There's a bakery too.

Connections

BUSES - frequent Mon-Sat link with Marlborough. Tel: 08457 090 899.
TRAINS - First Great Western provide a useful local service running to/from London Paddington providing incremental succour for towpath walkers. Tel: 08457 484950.

Little Bedwyn (Map 13)

St Michael's Church is built of local flint and completes a charming scene. The HARROW INN (Tel: 01672 870871) is a sophisticated restaurant and bar as opposed to a village local. "No draught beer and no bar snacks" but a mouthwatering menu none the less.

Hungerford (Map 14)

Hungerford's broad, sloping High Street strides confidently down to the canal, concealing the fact that the town is comparatively small. Nevertheless, it comes alive at least once a year on the occasion of the 'Hocktide Ceremony' (held on the second Tuesday following Easter) whereupon ninety-nine commoners are summoned to the Town Hall by the blowing of a horn. Two 'Tuttimen' are elected and proceed from house to house exchanging oranges for kisses. All very weird and wonderful!

Eating & Drinking

TUTTI POLE - adjacent Bridge 84. Coffees, lunches and teas served by a bevy of attentive and comely waitresses in traditional surroundings. Tel: 01488 682515.
THE BEAR - Charnham Street (north of Bridge 84) Tel: 01488 682512. Comfortable hotel offering bar and restaurant food. Elizabeth I and William of Orange have stayed here, and you should have seen the bill for their mini-bars.
CASANOVA - Charnham Street. Tel: 01488 682588. Italian restaurant and pizza house on A4 to north of canal.
AZUZA - High Street. Tel: 01488 644643. Baguettes and paninis in stylish modern coffee shop; nice courtyard tables.
THE DOWN GATE - Park Street. Charming pub on the edge of Hungerford Common, well worth a 15 minute walk. Tel: 01488 682708. Arkells ales from Swindon and a good choice of food.

Shopping

Disappointing in terms of individual food shops, Hungerford has become something of a centre for the antiques trade, BELOW STAIRS (up past the railway bridge on the High Street) being a typical example of this new focus of commerce.

HUNGERFORD BOOKSHOP (just past the Italianate Town Hall) is excellent for both new and secondhand titles. AFRICAN TRACKWORKS, again on High St., manufacture furniture from reclaimed Zimbabwean railway sleepers! More prosaically, there is a SOMERFIELD supermarket adjacent to the railway station, whilst if it's time to freshen up your undies, you'll find a handy launderette towards the top of the High Street.

Connections

TRAINS - First Great Western services along the Kennet corridor. Tel: 08457 484950.
BUSES - useful links with Swindon and Marlborough. Tel: 0870 608 2 608.

Kintbury (Map 15)

A delightful village with a notable church within which a tablet commemorates Charles Dundas, noting that he represented the County of Berks in 'ten successive Parliaments in full possession of every faculty'!

Eating & Drinking

DUNDAS ARMS - canalside Bridge 75. Tel: 01488 658263. Much loved waterside inn named after the first Chairman of the Kennet & Avon Company. Ramsbury ales from Marlborough; West Berkshire beers from Thatcham. Good food and accommodation.

Shopping

Londis convenience store and (astonishingly!) a fishmonger who dabbles additionally in seasonal game.

Connections

TRAINS - local First Great Western services along the Kennet Valley, very useful for towpath walks. Tel: 08457 484950.

Bosky Moorings Burghfield

30

Newbury Lock
& Town Bridge

Ham Lock

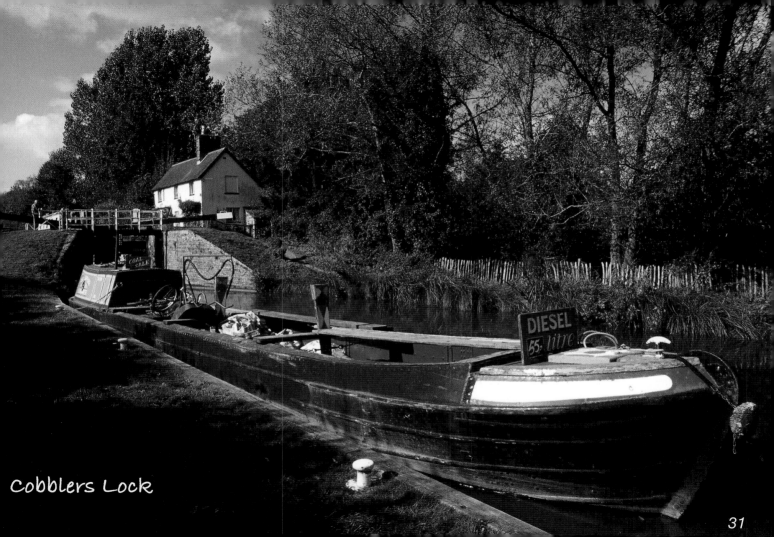

Cobblers Lock

FROXFIELD - where Wiltshire gives way to Royal Berkshire - once boasted a wharf and a feeder. Little remains of the former, but the feeder still enters the canal just below Froxfield Bottom Lock. Bridge 90 offers access to Froxfield village which boasts a remarkable group of almshouses known as the Duchess of Somerset's Hospital.

A change of county brings a change of mood as the A4 trunk road comes alongside the waterway to shake it out of its sleepy complacency. Fortunately, however, much of the A4's traffic has been siphoned off by the parallel M4 and it's not as fearfully busy as it once was. In any case, the K&A maintains its dignity as it makes its unruffled way eastwards accompanied by the River Dun which it crosses on a compact three-arched aqueduct above Cobbler's Lock.

Hungerford Marsh Lock is equipped with a swing bridge across the lock chamber, making it unique on the Kennet & Avon Canal and unusual even on the wider inland waterway system. The bridge was provided for the benefit of the commoners who enjoyed - and for that matter still do - rights over Freeman's Marsh, across which the canal journeys in company with the River Dun and the railway.

Hungerford's canalscape is immensely pleasing, a number of the wharfside buildings having been sympathetically restored for residential use. For well over a hundred years the wharf was occupied by J. Wooldridge & Son, builders, who were also responsible, from 1851-63, for the maintenance of the K&A between Wootton Rivers and Reading. They finally left the site in 1962. The present incumbents are ducks, swans, picnickers and a K&A Canal Trust trip boat.

In tandem with the crystal clear waters of the River Dun, the K&A crosses Hungerford Common, where commoners rights were granted by John O' Gaunt, father of King Henry IV, back in the fourteenth century. At Dun Mill Lock, confluence of the Dun and the Kennet, a couple of former mills have been converted into highly desirable residences. See how clear the Kennet is here. Further downstream, as it becomes navigable, turbidity becomes a problem, in other words you can't see the bottom from the top. Anglers believe that this is caused by diesel-powered boats whose propellers disturb the silt and bring an unwelcome opacity to the water that inhibits weed growth and affects fish stocks. It would be sad if this proved true.

A338 to Andover   For details of facilities at Hungerford turn back to page 29

RECONCEPTIONS that the best scenery belongs to the K&A west of Hungerford, and that it continues to get better the further you travel, are belied by the beauty of the Kennet's watermeadows. This is a mouthwatering length of navigation, as tasty as the watercress once grown in the extensive beds bordering the waterway between Hungerford and Kintbury, and punted downstream for onward transportation by rail. The cress farm has long since disappeared - overwhelmed by competition from the large growers in Hampshire and Dorset - and this is now the territory of the solitary angler and towpath walker.

Travelling eastbound, canal users encounter the capricious currents of the River Kennet for the first time. It was at Kintbury in June 1797 that the first section of the K&A was officially opened by its then chairman Charles Dundas, who was present to greet a military band transported along the cut from Newbury specifically for the jollifications. For a hundred years or so Kintbury Wharf thrived, handling large quantities of iron and coke destined for several local ironworks, as well as raw materials for the nearby brewery. Following

the canal's commercial decline and subsequent restoration, Kintbury took centre stage again in December 1972 when Miss W. Rennie, a descendant of John Rennie, officially reopened Kintbury Lock. This stretch of canal appeared (quite authentically!) in the novelist Robert Goddard's thriller *Sight Unseen*.

Untroubled by the outside world, the canal glides cheerily along in a world of its own, past the sublime slopes of The Wilderness and Irish Hill. The latter was once the site of a curious industry, chalk from the hill being gathered for the manufacture of whiting, a powder used in the production of paint. There were at one time five whiting mills in the Kintbury area, which sent their finished products along the canal to Bristol until the 1930s.

Those familiar with the music of Gerald Finzi might find it entering their heads. Finzi lived at Ashmansworth to the south of Newbury and founded the Newbury String Players during the Second World War. His very measured and lyrically English compositions inevitably find a resonance amidst the beauty of the Kennet Valley and its watermeadows.

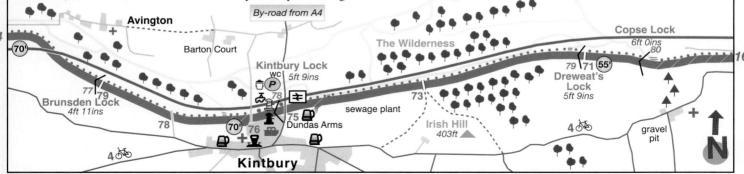

For details of facilities at Kintbury turn back to page 29

By-roads to Hamstead Marshall

THE Newbury Bypass, once the most infamous stretch of road in Britain, finally opened for business in November 1998, sixty two years after it was first mooted. The eight miles of new road took three years to build, cost a staggering £100 million (plus 10,000 ancient and mature trees) and resulted in the arrest of 1,014 people, including protesters, private security guards and contractors. The net effect of the bypass has been to cut journey times between the South Coast and the Midlands by an average of five minutes, whilst the volume of traffic in Newbury, although reduced in the short term, is expected to return to its pre-bypass level within ten years.

Ponder these facts and figures as you make your way beneath the new road bridge, its impact on the canal emphasised by the scenic splendour of nearby Hamstead Park, Enborne Copse and Benham Broad, the latter being an artificial lake created during the canal's construction to placate the Earl of Craven. But, for the canal traveller at least, the new bypass is but a temporary blot on the landscape and better things lie in store as Newbury reaches out to embrace the K&A. First though you pass beneath the Lambourn Valley Railway bridge, which carried trains of the LVR between Lambourn and Newbury from April 1898 until closure of the passenger service in January 1960. And there you have it - UK transport policy summed up perfectly during a ten-minute saunter along the towpath of the K&A: close railways and build roads.

Newbury is as welcoming as a log fire on a winter's evening. Indeed, it's difficult to think of any other town of comparable size which enhances a canal journey so comprehensively. If you're Reading bound the attractions begin at West Mills, where a swing bridge, a row of picturesque cottages (once a 17th century weaving factory) and the mill's surviving silo

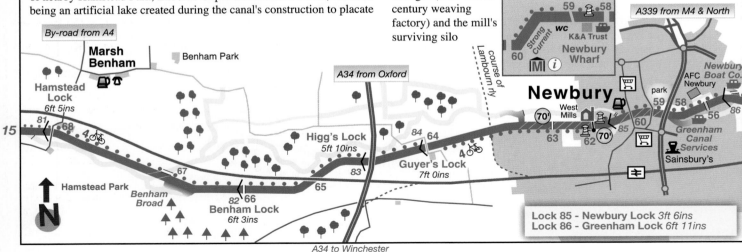

Lock 85 - Newbury Lock *3ft 6ins*
Lock 86 - Greenham Lock *6ft 11ins*

(tastefully converted into flats) combine to create a canalscape of picture postcard beauty. But Newbury hasn't always been the commuter town it is today. It was an important cloth-making centre in the fifteenth century and down the centuries manufacturing and commerce played important roles in the town's development. West Mills Wharf was once a hive of activity, handling, amongst other commodities, coal from the Somerset collieries. Its last commercial use came in 1950 when a cargo of salt from Middlewich was delivered by John Knill. Newbury Lock was the first to be completed, in 1796, on the Newbury-Bath section of the canal. Unique on the K&A, it is equipped with lever-operated ground paddles of a type relatively common on northern canals, where they are referred to as cloughs. Beside the lock a small plaque, unveiled in 1997, pays tribute to the late John Gould MBE, founder member of the Kennet & Avon Canal Trust and former working boatman, who died in March 1999. "Without him there would be no K&A Canal."

Ambushed by the lively waters of the Kennet and a mill stream that enters from the opposite side, the navigation proceeds under Town Bridge - a stylish, single-arched stone structure dating from 1770. Being the terminus of the original Kennet Navigation, it was built without a towpath, which presented problems for horse-drawn craft, especially as it was forbidden for horses to haul across the main road. The solution involved a special float, kept by the lock; whilst the barge was tied below the bridge and the horse by the lock, the float was attached to the tow rope and allowed to drift down below the bridge to the barge. Then once the horse started pulling the barge would move through the bridge and into the lock: the natural flow downstream normally being sufficient to carry the vessel through the bridge. Moorings are provided at Victoria Park (although we consider West Mills to be the nicest place to spend the night), directly opposite Newbury Wharf. Originally the terminal wharf of the Kennet Navigation, this was one of the busiest wharves on the K&A, but most of it disappeared under, in chronological order, a bus station, car park and the main Inner Relief road. The two-storeyed Stone Wharf Building survives, however, and serves as K&A Canal Trust branch headquarters, shop and small museum.

Newbury   (Map 16)

Few towns successfully embrace the inland waterways on their doorstep as comprehensively as Newbury. The navigation passes through the very heart of the town, whereas most communities tend to keep their distance from so vulgar a hinterland. Northbrook Street, the main shopping thoroughfare, is carried across the navigation enabling a quick shop to be done while your boat is worked through Newbury Lock. Look out for the imposing church of St Nicholas built in the 16th century by a wealthy Newbury wool merchant. On 25th June 1811, in a demonstration of 'manufacturing celerity' the celebrated 'Newbury Coat' was tailored from wool shorn in the morning from two sheep and worn by Sir John Throckmorton 13 hours and 20 minutes later.

Eating & Drinking

LOCK STOCK & BARREL - Bridge 60. Tel: 01635 42730. Lively modern Fullers (of Chiswick) pub with waterside terrace.
PREZZO - Cheap Street. Tel: 01635 31957. Contemporary Italian in converted Carnegie Library between the Market Place and the railway station.

Shopping

An amenable town to shop in with all facilities very close to the canal. Don't miss the opportunity to purchase some Newbury Sausage from GRIFFINS butchers overlooking Bridge 60. Markets on Thursdays and Saturdays. Really good secondhand bookshop (INVICTA - Tel: 01635 31176) in Cromwell Place (off Northbrook Street opp M&S). The Kennet Shopping Mall features Debenhams, Laura Ashley et al.

Things to Do

TOURIST INFORMATION - The Wharf. Tel: 01635 30267.
WEST BERKSHIRE MUSEUM - The Wharf. Tel: 01635 30511. Excellent local museum housed in former cloth hall and granary.

Connections

TRAINS - First Great Western offer excellent services along the Kennet Valley. Tel: 08457 484950.
BUSES - services supplement the trains along the Kennet Valley but additionally operate to tantalisingly remote villages up on the downs. Tel: 0870 608 2 608.
TAXIS - Cabco. Tel: 01635 33333.

LOCKS come fairly frequently as the canal makes its way secretively between Newbury and Thatcham. Breezes sigh through the bullrushes with the provocative rustle that petticoats used to make. Business parks (Newbury is Vodafone's global headquarters) and the railway ensure that the canal traveller has no cognisance of the town's famous racing course. Could the old heavy-treading boat-horses sense the presence of thoroughbreds nearby, and were they envious of these equine cousins' gilded lifestyles?

Gradually, time is erasing Greenham's synonymy with nuclear missiles and it's all too easy to forget the mass protests and the Women's Peace Camp, all of which was acted out less than a mile south of the K&A. The area north of the canal is an important ecological site where reed and sedge warblers and rare butterflies thrive in a unique lake and reed bed environment; the Nature

Discovery Centre, located close to Widmead Lock, offers the chance to explore this fascinating terrain along a number of designated paths.

At just over a mile, the Long Cut is the longest straight on the entire K&A. The cut leads on to Monkey Marsh Lock, ostensibly one of the last remaining examples of the turf-sided locks once prevalent on the Kennet Navigation. These had timber walled chambers to some two feet above the lock's lower level, above which their turf sides sloped away at an angle of 45 degrees. Whilst the locks were filling there was considerable water loss through the turf banks but copious supplies of water from the Kennet meant that this was not considered a problem. Sadly, Monkey Marsh Lock has been inappropriately restored with copious use of concrete and steel, an ugly compromise, leaving one to suspect that the sensible precepts of health and safety are being allowed to over-indulge themselves, probably out of an inbred fear of insurance claim and counter-claim.

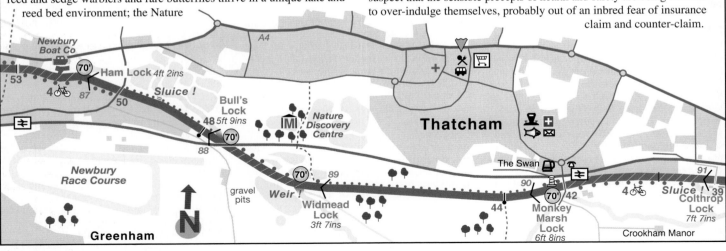

36

Thatcham (Map 17)

A lengthy walk through suburbia faces the canal traveller intent on visiting the fleshpots of Thatcham. Closer at hand, however, is a good pub, whilst a few minutes further on are a row of shops providing most of life's necessities (paracetamol and fish & chips for example). But if you feel like stretching your legs, Thatcham does evince a curious post Sixties charm about its town square. Almost the only building left of any antiquity is the church, though even that was 'violently restored' in 1852 according to Betjeman & Piper's *Architectural Guide to Berkshire*. A Millennium monument in the square salutes some of Thatcham's significant events, such as the arrival of electric light in 1920, the first telephone in 1912, and the Kennet Navigation in 1723, whilst, in 1160, Thatcham Market was attacked by a band of brigands from Newbury. Stirring stuff!

Eating & Drinking

SWAN HOTEL - Station Road. Tel: 01635 862084. Food and accommodation. *Further pubs in the town centre, whilst Thatcham seems to have more fish & chip shops than a northern mill town, the nearest being just 5 minutes walk from Bridge 42. Also in the town centre are several ethnic restaurants and takeaways.*

Shopping

There's an 'Alldays' general store within 5 minutes of the canal as well as a pharmacist and post office. All the main high street banks have branches in the town centre where you'll also find a Waitrose supermarket and even a small bookshop. Best of all, however, is WYATTS butchers & fishmongers shop - a real find.

Connections

BUSES - Newbury Buses link the town centre with Newbury and Reading. Tel: 0870 608 2 608. *Services 1/2 offer a 30 minute frequency connection between the railway station and the town centre.*

TRAINS - First Great Western services to/from Newbury and Reading with useful stops at Midgham and Theale for towpath users. Tel: 08457 484950.

Woolhampton (Map 18)

Former coaching village on the old Bath Road, suffering demolition when the road was widened. Douai Abbey can be accessed to the North.

Eating & Drinking

ROW BARGE - canalside, Bridge 31. Tel: 0118 971 2213. Ubiquitous freehouse with extensive beer garden overlooking the navigation. Bar food, BBQs, Greene King ales.

FALMOUTH ARMS - Bath Road (village centre) - Tel: 0118 971 3202. Friendly local offering food, families welcome. B&B.

THE ANGEL - Bath Road. Beautifully appointed restaurant which may dent your plastic but with a concomitant rise in morale. Tel: 0118 971 3307.

Shopping

Small newsagency dealing also in sandwiches, pies and sausage rolls: open daily, mornings only on Sundays. Tiny Post Office. Well stocked garage shop on A4 to east.

Connections

TRAINS - First Great Western trains. Remember that the station is called 'Midgham' ! Tel: 08457 484950.

Aldermaston Wharf (Map 19)

Aldermaston itself lies a country mile to the south-west along the A340 but the wharf itself is worth lingering over and you should start with British Waterways' VISITOR CENTRE (Tel: 0118 971 2868) which was originally a canal employee's cottage. A short waymarked trail will introduce you to Aldermaston Wharf's salient features including: the former transhipment arm, the lock, the lift-bridge, and the remains of an old brewery. Refreshments and gifts are also available at the visitor centre.

Eating & Drinking

BUTT INN - a few hundred yards south of the canal at Aldermaston Bridge. Tel: 0118 971 2129. Bar meals, families welcome, garden.

Connections

TRAINS - First Great Western trains. Local services linking Newbury with Reading. Tel: 08457 484950.

Theale (Map 19)

Quainter than Thatcham, and not such a long walk from the canal, Theale has a friendly air about it and an adequate choice of shops. Its church is an imposing example of Gothic revival which includes interior work by Bodley.

Eating & Drinking

CUMBERS - High Street. Tel: 0118 930 2405. Succulent hot sandwiches etc to take-away. *Lots of pubs and Thai and Chinese restaurants also.*

Shopping

Co-op, pharmacy, newsagent, post office, bakery and Lloyds TSB bank all located on the High Street seven or eight minutes stroll from the canal.

Connections

TRAINS - trains link stations along the canal from Reading to Newbury. Tel: 08457 484950.

LOW-LYING, yet well-wooded, the navigation exudes great charm as it continues its undemonstrative way through the Kennet Valley. To the north, Bucklebury Common rises to over four hundred feet; to the south Crookham Common is almost as high: both form rewarding - not to say tempting - horizons.

The railway remains a constant companion, its passenger expresses and locals leavened by lengthy goods trains carrying Wiltshire-quarried stone to the construction company stockpiles of Greater London. Incidentally, the Great Western Railway years ago renamed the little station on Woolhampton's doorstep 'Midgham', concerned lest Woolhampton be confused with Wolverhampton, the Black Country industrial centre north of Birmingham! To the north, prominent on the skyline, stands Midgham's lonely Victorian church.

Swing-bridges abound: No.31, at Woolhampton, deserves care and attention when approached from upstream as, below the tail of the lock, the river makes a brisk entrance, and you must have your wits about you if you are not to be the cause of merriment (at best or *schadenfreude* at worst) amongst the patrons of the adjoining beer garden. Electrified now, the bridge poses no inherent problems in operation, but reflect that, in

1940, Tom and Angela Rolt took three hours to negotiate their way past the bridge with the help of 'half the able-bodied men of the village heaving on crow-bars under the direction of the red-faced landlord of the Row Barge. On the same journey, the locks were in equally recalcitrant condition, and the Rolts were grateful for an abundance of reeds, bunches of which they heaved into the lock chambers to staunch the flow of water from heavily leaking gates. An earlier traveller and writer to explore the K&A had been Fred S. Thacker, whose book *Kennet Country* was published by Blackwells of Oxford in 1932. He and his wife voyaged along the navigation in 1919, even then not without difficulty, both mechanical and bureaucratic: 'It has cost me some weeks of negotiation with the railway company, and an initial outlay of twenty shillings to obtain a permit to enter the Kennet.'

Halfway along the picturesquely wooded interlude between bridges 30 and 29, the Kennet leaves the canal and heads off in the direction of Aldermaston, being navigable, for those of a curious disposition, at least as far as Frouds Bridge Marina, if not Aldermaston Mill which once received its grain by barge.

For details of facilities at Woolhampton turn back to page 37

SILICON chip business parks may embower the A4, but the Kennet & Avon keeps its head down, remaining remote and unruffled, marching past Aldermaston Wharf in its own silent protest at progress and man's inhumanity, not so much to man, as to the landscape.

Long before the era of the nuclear protest marches, the Great Western Railway inserted an arm off the main channel of the canal to facilitate interchange between rail and water. It paralleled the railway for some distance but most of it was infilled at the outset of the Second World War - doubtless some top brass tactician foresaw the Third Reich commandeering the arm to further its strategic advance across southern Britain. We may scorn from the sophistication of the 21st century, but fear makes fools of us all, and are we not equally irrational now in the face of terrorism? Try finding a litter bin at a railway station and you have the answer.

In point of fact, the military identified the K&A as a Blue Defence Line. Pill boxes were installed at numerous locations. According to Rolt: 'The last of the Kennet & Avon boatmen was dragged from retirement and put in charge of a leaking maintenance boat hauled by a

broken-down horse led by a dim-witted youth'. Ere long, the vessel, overloaded by inexperienced squaddies, sank and put a summary end to the proceedings. Our good friend, George Behrend (author of that peerless railway book *Gone With Regret*) recalls tank practice in the vicinity of the canal, and an altercation with a senior officer who refused to accept that the average K&A swingbridge was not necessarily designed to bear the weight of a tank. On a hillside to the north, beyond the A4, Englefield House catches the eye from the pound between Tyle Mill and Sulhamstead locks. Researching this length one wintry day, we came upon horses splashing through floodwater in fields neighbouring the navigation like something out of the Camargue. Even in monochrome, and with foreshortened horizons, we could sense how beautiful the K&A could be at any time of the year, never mind its dragonfly-filled summers. Ufton Lock has disappeared. It was only shallow in any case, a mere 1ft 9ins, provided in the 1830s to give greater depth below Towney Lock. Towney was rebuilt as part of the restoration programme in 1974, and associated improvements rendered Ufton obsolete.

A4 from Newbury

Aldermaston Wharf

18

95

Idermaston Lock
6ft 11ins

97

Visitor Centre
Reading Marine

Padworth Lock
5ft 1in
70'

28

96 27

26 Towney Lock
9ft 8ins

R. Kennet

25

70'

site of Ufton Lock

Spring Mill

Tyle Mill

WC

Weir !

Tyle Mill Lock
6ft 4ins

99 23

70'

Weir !

Sulhamstead

21

100

Sulhamstead Lock
4ft 1in

70'

Theale

A4 to London

19 101 **20**

Sheffield Lock
2ft 2ins

P

Sulhamstead

By-road to Padworth · *For details of facilities at Aldermaston Wharf and Theale turn back to page 37* · By-roads to Burghfield

39

HE M4 motorway impinges briefly. You can marvel at its ugliness. One day it will be grass-grown, nothing is more certain. And then we will love it, wondering at the romance of its heyday.

As for the K&A you will be either conscious of its impending end or coming slowly to terms with its prosaic beginnings in a gravel pit flawed landscape. Keep the faith, back in 1919 Fred S. Thacker slaked his thirst at the Cunning Man (whose landlord didn't know the source of its name) discovered 'alluring lanes' leaving for Binfield, Grazeley and Shinfield and quickly learnt that a voyage along the Kennet 'is very delightful'.

Garston Lock is essentially the sole remaining turf-sided chamber (see Map 17) and one can't help thinking that the pillboxes overlooking it are there to protect it from that Fifth Columnist called Progress. At Bridge 17 the towpath changes sides and the National Cycle Route No.4 detours off to the south, passing former gravel workings now adopted by Theale Water Skiing Club. Burghfield Lock - and, indeed, all the original twenty turf-sided locks between Reading and Newbury - originally dates from between 1715 and 1724, but was enlarged in the 1760s to accept the massive 'Newbury' barges which measured 19ft in the beam and 109ft in length and could carry a cargo of over a

hundred tons. The lock chamber in use now dates from the early years of restoration and was ceremoniously opened by the Chairman of British Waterways in 1968.

There were osier beds beside the canal between bridges 15 and 14. They were once harvested for basket making. Burghfield Island provides popular private moorings away from the main navigable channel under the aegis of the Burghfield Island Boat Club. Seven and a half thousand new dwellings are due to be erected in Burghfield in the foreseeable future!

Downstream of Southcote Lock the railway line from Reading to Basingstoke crosses the navigation. An important link between the midlands and the south, there are frequent Virgin Voyagers and a considerable amount of container traffic making its way to and from Southampton Docks, making one wish there was still a residue of commercial traffic on the Kennet & Avon. Fobney Lock is overlooked by Reading's waterworks, pumping station and filter beds.

Eating & Drinking
THE CUNNING MAN - canalside Bridge 14. Tel: 0118 960 7010. Large, family-orientated, all-day canalside pub with garden

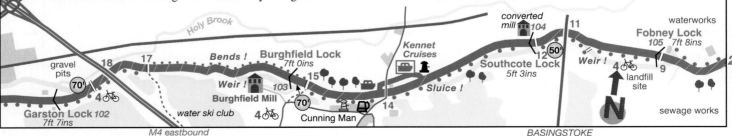

R EADING forms the pivotal point in this guidebook. Here we exchange the rather less celebrated (though hardly less charismatic) Kennet & Avon for the regal Thames, or vice versa. The two waterways' passage through the county town of Berkshire could hardly be more contrasting: the Kennet hemmed in by an urban backdrop and a high tech retail zone; the Thames wide and spacious. By most standards, however, the retail park, rejoicing in the confident title of 'The Oracle', makes successful use of the navigation, incorporating it to a higher degree than most other examples we have met on our inland waterway travels: though mooring in the immediate vicinity is prohibited on account of deep water and fast currents. From the glass fronted House of Fraser cafe, Reading's shoppers regard passing boaters with jaw-dropping awe, perhaps in the sudden realisation that retail therapy can't compete with canal travel in the final analysis.

Eastbound, County Lock is the last under British Waterways' jurisdiction, boaters proceed under traffic light control from here owing to the narrow nature of the channel ahead, one-way operation being the order of the day. The strength of the current is often increased by the narrow nature of the channel, westbound you may notice that your boat is making heavy weather of its progress; eastbound, don't get carried away!

Simonds Brewery overlooked the Kennet from 1789 onwards until the business was bought out by Courage in 1960 and, typically, closed a dozen years later. The navigation here was known as the 'Brewery Gut', and it was both deep and dangerous. As at Newbury, the absence of a towpath made difficult working practices for horse-drawn barges. At one point a line was attached to a pulley and the boat horse given a sharp smack on its hindquarters which had the effect of propelling the barge in to the bridgehole. Further on a long length of rope was floated down the navigation and attached to the barge, which had to be hauled a further two hundred yards from the bank. Ponder on these archaic working practices as you watch

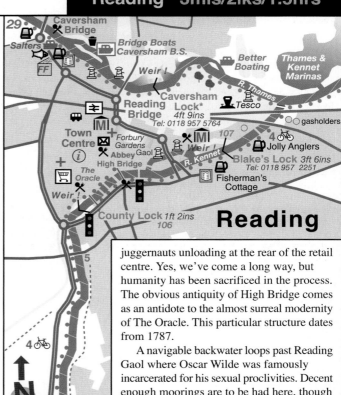

juggernauts unloading at the rear of the retail centre. Yes, we've come a long way, but humanity has been sacrificed in the process. The obvious antiquity of High Bridge comes as an antidote to the almost surreal modernity of The Oracle. This particular structure dates from 1787.

A navigable backwater loops past Reading Gaol where Oscar Wilde was famously incarcerated for his sexual proclivities. Decent enough moorings are to be had here, though we would continue to labour the point that local authorities rarely appear to put the red carpet out for waterborne visitors. Huntley &

continued overleaf

Palmer's biscuit factory overlooked this stretch of water. Only one brick building converted into flats remains of what was in its heyday a twenty-four acre site with six thousand employees producing over two hundred varieties of tinned biscuits. The new Prudential Building occupies much of this, a charmless landmark symbolic of industrial change. Up until the Second World War water transport was used both to bring flour in to Huntley & Palmers and take finished biscuits out, many destined for morale-boosting export to outposts of the Empire via London Docks. A dense network of terraced streets lay to the south of the Kennet to house H&P's workforce.

Blakes Lock is operated by the Environment Agency and evinces all the characteristics of a Thames lock. Licences can be purchased from the keeper for use of the Thames and/or the Kennet & Avon if your boat is not already so equipped. Blake's Lock is said to be named after an 18th Century Mayor of Reading who opposed construction of the Kennet & Avon Canal - we can only be grateful that he didn't get his way.

Gasholders and railway bridges mark the confluence of the Kennet with the Thames. The roving bridge here dates from 1892, prior to which watermen and their horses were carried across the mouth of the river by ferry boat. Not the most romantic of backdrops, but adrenalin is likely to be running in any boater or walker making the transition - it always does at inland waterway junctions, whatever their nature.

Reading   *(Maps 21 & 30)*

In common with the likes of Northampton and Stafford, Reading tends to be thought of as a County Town that is superficially uninspiring. In all three cases nothing could be further from the truth. Squeezed between the Thames and the Kennet, Reading exudes brash overtones of London, but manages to retain the atmosphere of Berkshire. Should one slacken one's gait on Broad Street, the handsome main thoroughfare softened by plane trees, one is pestered by religious zealots and market researchers with the assiduousness of merchants in a kasbah. Avoid eye contact at all cost, lift up your gaze instead to the terracotta embellishments of Reading's Edwardian shops, and seek out the quieter oases of calm as manifested by Forbury Gardens (where the Mainwand Lion commemorates over three hundred members of the Berkshire Regiment lost in the Afghan War of the 1880s) and the Abbey ruins. Two churches deserve notice: St Laurence-in-Reading and St Mary the Virgin, the latter with a chequerboard tower of flint and limestone. In

Caversham Bridge

the 18th century Wiltshire stone was carried down the Kennet to build a crescent reminiscent of Bath on Queen's Road which runs parallel to the south of the canal east of High Bridge.

Eating & Drinking

BEL & THE DRAGON - Gasworks Road. Tel: 0118 951 5790. Charming contemporary restaurant & bar located alongside the Riverside Museum upstream of Blakes Lock. Sophisticated and secure 'fishbone' customer moorings lend it added appeal, and apparently the owners are keen boaters themselves.

LONDON STREET BRASSERIE - High Bridge. Tel: 0118 950 5036. Stylish modern restaurant with terrace overlooking the navigation. NINO'S - Market Place. Tel: 0118 958 8966. Authentic and homely little Italian restaurant. LOCH FYNE - Fobney Street (opposite County Lock). Tel: 0118 918 5850. Seafood restaurant and bar. Breakfasts, lunches and dinners. FISHERMAN'S COTTAGE - Kennet Side (by Blakes Lock). Tel: 0118 957 1553. Food and Fuller's beer in convivial canalside pub. THREE MEN IN A BOAT - Caversham Bridge. Tel: 0118 925 9988. Restaurant & bar adjunct to Crown Plaza Hotel. Riverside terrace. ISLAND - Caversham Bridge. Tel: 0118 948 4573. Pavilion like restaurant/bar on the Thames. PREZZO - Minster Street. Tel: 0118 959 6092. Growing (and reliable) chain of Italian restaurants. HOBGOBLIN - Broad Street. Tel: 0118 950 8119. *Good Beer Guide* recommended serious drinker's den featuring three West Berkshire Brewery beers plus guests.

continued on page 61

The River Thames

Cliveden Reach

OWN and Gown may define the City of Oxford's personality split, but the gulf is echoed by its canal and its river: the former self-effacing and humdrum, the latter exhibitionist and haughty. Access between these contrasting inland waterways is by way of the Sheepwash Channel, spanned by the main railway line into Oxford from the north and overlooked by new housing. Upstream the Thames remains navigable as far as Lechlade, a delightful route covered effusively in the *Severn, Avon & Cotswold Canal Companion.*

Via Osney Lock the Thames traverses the western periphery of Oxford, re-encountering the railway and passing beneath a sturdy bridge of iron construction which once carried a siding into the gasworks - even the Thames can be mundanely functional when duty calls. But for most residents and visitors the Thames at Oxford manifests itself most obviously at Folly Bridge where punts are available for hire and Salter's faded yet still elegant 'steamers' can still be taken throughout the summer season in stages downstream to Staines.

One wonders if it is the undergraduates or the tourists who take to punting nowadays, it seems too sentimental an activity for modern youth. Yet the college rowing clubs obviously continue to flourish, even if their stately barges have been for the most part replaced by club houses with a firm grasp of terra firma. With your gaze attracted by these sizeable establishments you might miss the gentle ingress of the Cherwell, Oxford's most ethereal watercourse. More business like, the Thames negotiates the typically picturesque Iffley Lock, already establishing, for downstream newcomers, its capacity for escaping the less salubrious aspects of its mundane hinterland. Iffley is famed (by the cognoscenti at least) for the quality of its Norman church. The equally appealing Old Parsonage, whose garden runs idyllically down to the Thames, is available for let through the estimable Landmark Trust - Tel: 01628 825920.

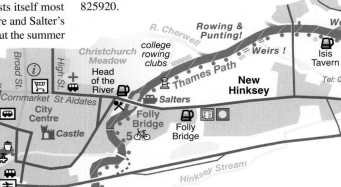

*Figures relate to Thames downstream of Osney Bridge

Oxford (Map 22)

Oxford's pressures seem not so much 'Town & Gown' nowadays, as 'Town & Tourism'. Yet it can still remind you of an exclusive club, where the best the casual visitor can do is press their nose up against the lattice windowpane and peer enviously at the academically privileged world revealed within. Like Thomas Hardy's hero, we are all 'Obscure Judes', in awe of this world-renowned seat of learning. In Oxford - perhaps more than in any other English city - time stands quite literally still. Whole quadrangles and cloisters seem frozen into a medieval eternity where only the undergraduates ubiquitous bicycles break the chronological spell. From the perspective of the river boat, or the open-topped tourist bus, the sightseer can derive a vicarious wisdom. After all, you can now truthfully recall: "When I was at Oxford ..."

Eating & Drinking

ISIS TAVERN - riverside above Iffley Lock. Tel: 01865 247006. Isolated yet popular riverside inn which used to have its beer delivered by barge. Moorings nearby.

KING'S ARMS - Sandford Lock. Popular riverside pub offering bar and restaurant meals. Families welcome. Tel: 01865 777095.

HEAD OF THE RIVER - Folly Bridge. Tel: 01865 721600. Lively conversion of former grain warehouse. Fullers ales, waterside terrace.

AZIZ PANDESIA - Folly Bridge. Tel: 01865 247775. Asian fusion food in sophisticated surroundings which include a floating terrace on the Thames.

FOLLY BRIDGE - Abingdon Road. Tel: 01865 790106. Cheerfully basic Wadworth house offering value food a few hundred yards south of Folly Bridge.

WATERMANS ARMS - riverside above Osney Lock. Tel: 01865 248832. Cosy local, bar food.

LE PETIT BLANC - Walton Street. Tel: 01865 510999. Raymond Blanc owned restaurant hidden away in the backstreets of Jericho and celebrating its tenth anniversary in 2006.

SHANGHAI 30's - St Aldates. Formerly the highly regarded Restaurant Elizabeth, now a Chinese. Tel: 01865 242230.

Shopping

Drawing on a wide range of custom and taste, Oxford's shops are inspired to an admirable eclecticism. The COVERED MARKET (off High Street) hosts the most wonderful cross-section of retailers and those who have travelled the length and breadth of this guide from Bristol will find a resemblance to the market there. As befits a seat of learning, there are some good bookshops, though not, sadly, as many secondhand and antiquarian outlets as we seem to remember.

Things to Do

TOURIST INFORMATION - Broad Street. Tel: 01865 726871 *www.visitoxford.org*

CITY SIGHTSEEING - open top bus rides with running commentary. Regular departures from the railway station and city centre stops. Tel: 01865 790522.

OXFORD CASTLE - New Road. Tel: 01865 260666. Redevelopment on historic castle site of former gaol. Many well known brand eating establishments on the same location.

THE OXFORD STORY - Broad Street. Jorvik style ride through Oxford's rich history. Tel: 01865 728822.

MUSEUM OF OXFORD - St Aldates. Tel: 01865 815559.

ASHMOLEAN MUSEUM - Beaumont Street. Tel: 01865 278000. Britain's oldest public museum (not Mons) displaying European, Egyptian and Near Eastern antiquities.

CARFAX TOWER - Carfax. 99 steps to heaven for a bird's eye view of the city of dreaming spires.

PUNT HIRE - Oxford's most traditional means of seduction can be hired from boat houses at Folly Bridge on the Thames and Magdelan Bridge on the Cherwell.

COLLEGES - over thirty colleges make up Oxford University. Many of them are world famous such as Balliol and Merton which are both of 13th century origin; Magdalen (pronounced 'Maudlin') which dates from 1458; and Christ Church founded in 1525 by Cardinal Wolsey. The general (less well-educated) public may look around most of them in the afternoons.

OPEN SPACES - much of Oxford's charm rests in the proliferation of green spaces, the city's lungs. These include: The Parks, Christ Church Meadow and Port Meadow. A stroll - or a picnic -on any of them comes as a refreshing experience after the hurly burly of the main thoroughfares and helps put Oxford in the context of its riverside setting.

Connections

TRAINS - services along the Thames Valley to/from Reading and London and connections to/from the midlands and the north. Tel: 08457 484950.

BUSES - contact the Oxford Bus Company on 01865 785400 or Traveline on 0870 608 2 608.

Oxford College Rowing Clubs

The Thames at Iffley

Folly Bridge

PERHAPS even the Thames itself would admit to being at its most lacklustre between Iffley and Abingdon. In the reach below Sandford Lock especially it is characterised by accompanying scrubland and a plethora of electricity pylons. But these are minor lapses in concentration and quickly forgiven. Elsewhere on this stretch there is much to look out for and muse over. Kennington Railway Bridge carries the rump of the old line via Thame to Princes Risborough, and over it now - instead of a Prairie tank and a pair of superannuated carriages - run goods trains bearing Minis, freshly made at the motor works in nearby Cowley. This is *Progress,* we're assured. Another victim of time has been the paper mill at Sandford Lock, its former site occupied by housing now.

Narrowboats used to bring coal down from the Warwickshire coalfield to feed its hungry furnaces. Sandford, with an almost nine foot fall, is the deepest lock upstream of Teddington. Its origins can be traced back to 1632. In contrast, the lock-keeper's cottage dates from 1914.

Downstream of Radley College boathouse, shallow hills and woods redeem the anodyne reach above. Nuneham House overlooks the river and in its gracious grounds stands the Carfax Conduit, an artefact pertaining to Oxford's 17th century water supply rendered redundant by the widening of High Street in 1787. Not a great deal can be seen from the river of the house itself (in which Victoria and Albert honeymooned in 1841) but the grounds are the work of no lesser a gardener than 'Capability' Brown. Charles Dodgson (aka Lewis Carroll) used to row Alice Liddell down to Nuneham as an alternative to their more regular forays upstream to Godstow. Lock Wood Island recalls the existence of a lock at this point which ceased being used around 1800, at which time the channel changed from the east side to the west.

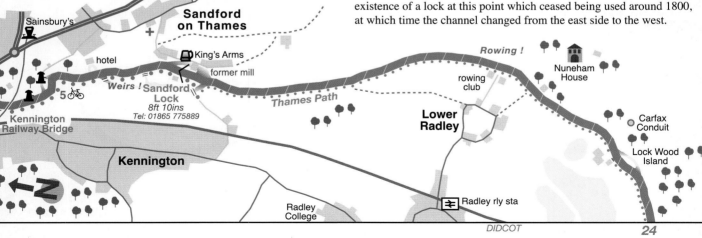

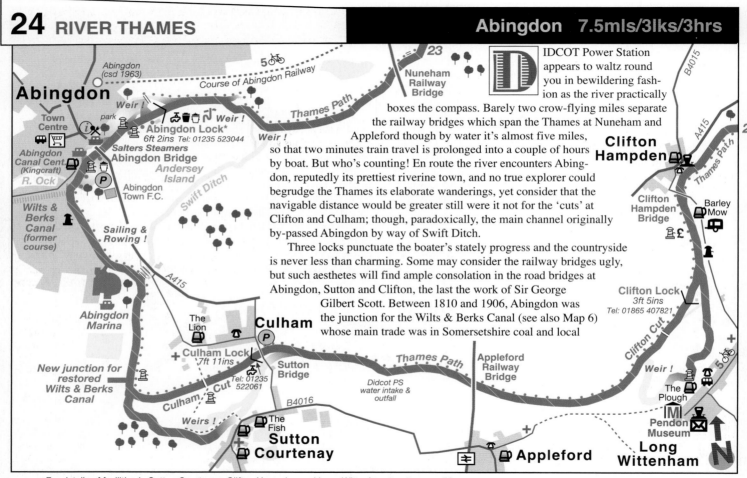

IDCOT Power Station appears to waltz round you in bewildering fashion as the river practically boxes the compass. Barely two crow-flying miles separate the railway bridges which span the Thames at Nuneham and Appleford though by water it's almost five miles, so that two minutes train travel is prolonged into a couple of hours by boat. But who's counting! En route the river encounters Abingdon, reputedly its prettiest riverine town, and no true explorer could begrudge the Thames its elaborate wanderings, yet consider that the navigable distance would be greater still were it not for the 'cuts' at Clifton and Culham; though, paradoxically, the main channel originally by-passed Abingdon by way of Swift Ditch.

Three locks punctuate the boater's stately progress and the countryside is never less than charming. Some may consider the railway bridges ugly, but such aesthetes will find ample consolation in the road bridges at Abingdon, Sutton and Clifton, the last the work of Sir George Gilbert Scott. Between 1810 and 1906, Abingdon was the junction for the Wilts & Berks Canal (see also Map 6) whose main trade was in Somersetshire coal and local

For details of facilities in Sutton Courtenay, Clifton Hampden and Long Wittenham turn to page 50

agricultural produce; although, ironically, it did prove useful in the movement of materials for construction of the Great Western Railway through the Vale of the White Horse. Unlike the Kennet & Avon, it was a narrowbeam canal, and this restriction certainly did it no favours with the advent of the Railway Age. Trade at the Abingdon end had all but evaporated in the 1880s and there is virtually no trace of the canal's junction with the Thames other than a slight indentation in the retaining wall above Wilsham Road, close to where the River Ock joins the main river beneath a little iron bridge bearing the misleading inscription: 'Wilts & Berks Canal 1824'. Abingdon might have become an inland waterway crossroads if the plan for a canal to Aylesbury had ever come to fruition. The enthusiastic Wilts & Berks Canal Trust continue to campaign for restoration of the canal, and have unveiled the beginnings of a new linking section to the south of Abingdon Marina.

Clifton Cut dates from 1822, and Culham Cut from 1809. Prior to their construction trade was hampered by flash locks and the use of the river by a watermill at Sutton Courtenay. Swift Ditch probably represented the original course of the river before Abingdon's monks diverted the channel past their abbey. In the 17th century Swift Ditch regained its importance as the main line of navigation and featured one of the earliest pound-locks in England. Around 1790, with the construction of a lock at Abingdon, Swift Ditch lost its status and became a backwater once again.

Appleford Railway Bridge dates from 1843 and its construction led to much debate between the Thames Commissioners and the Great Western Railway whose line approached the river from either direction on low-lying ground. A high bridge to facilitate the passage of masted vessels would have necessitated lengthy approach embankments which would have been detrimental to high speed running. The railway builders appear to have had things their way, for the bow span girder bridge stands only thirteen feet above water, the third lowest crossing on the whole river below Oxford.

Abingdon   (Map 24)

Excellent municipal moorings - provided, what's more, free of charge - can only add to the popularity of the 'Queen of the Thames', and Abingdon is an engaging town full of architectural, cultural and historical surprises. Pearsons would not be Pearsons, though, if we did not take umbrage at Abingdon's post 1974 transfer from Berkshire to Oxfordshire, the crass meddling of politicians and bureaucrats overturning the stabilities of centuries - reorganization for reorganization's sake. And there have been two well known commercial casualties - MG motor cars and the Morland brewery. That off our chests, we commend Abingdon to you and suggest that you see the remains of the Abbey, St Helen's high-spired, flying-buttressed church, and the amazing County Hall, a Wren-like building which has not unreasonably been declared 'the grandest town hall in England'.

Eating & Drinking

BROAD FACE - Bridge Street. Tel: 01235 524516. Broad faced and broad church in its award-winning approach to catering, this immensely appealing eating establishment close by Abingdon Bridge exudes style and quality. Attentive staff and an imaginative contemporary menu - try the Beef & Guinness Casserole served with potato and vegetable mash. Fish is also a speciality - the more esoteric likes of Marlin, Squid and Mullet featuring regularly. A good wine list is supplemented by Morland Bitter; (now brewed, alas, half-way across the country by Greene King in Bury St Edmunds) Fairtrade coffees and herbal teas.

UPPER REACHES - Thames Street. Tel: 01235 522311. High quality hotel offering meals to non residents in their Millwheel Restaurant & Brasserie immediately upstream of bridge where there are good moorings for patrons.

Shopping

A good place to shop if, in our opinion, not quite so relaxed as Wallingford. A modern precinct leads from the Market Place to a branch of Waitrose, and there is a Country Market every Friday.

Things to Do

TOURIST INFORMATION - Old Abbey House. Tel: 01235 522711 www.whitehorsedc.gov.uk
ABINGDON MUSEUM - County Hall, Market Place. Tel: 01235 523703. Worth visiting just to be in the beautiful building which houses it.

Connections

BUSES - Oxford Bus Co. Services X3/X4 offer a frequent daily link between Abingdon and Oxford city centre and railway station using state of the art air-conditioned Mercedes Benz buses. Services 32A & 35A operate southwards to Didcot Parkway railway station. Tel: 0870 608 2 608.
TAXIS - Auto-Taxi. Tel: 01235 524780.

Clifton Hampden (Map 24)

"Self-consciously picturesque" avowed John Piper in his 1938 *Shell Guide to Oxfordshire*, and you can still see what he meant. Sergeant William Dykes who accidentally began the Battle of Waterloo is buried in the churchyard. Post office stores.

Eating & Drinking

BARLEY MOW - riverside. This famous and popular inn ('the quaintest, most old-world inn up the river' according to JKJ) is now part of the Chef & Brewer chain. MG used to use its picturesque appearance as a backdrop for their publicity shots. Tel: 01865 407847. Moorings on opposite bank.

Long Wittenham (Map 24)

Backwaters always beguile, and moorings to the rear of The Plough offer every inducement to turn temporarily away from the main channel to explore the low-lying village of Long Wittenham. The predominantly Early English church is very pretty. Robert Gibbings, the engraver, and author of *Sweet Thames Run Softly* and its elegiac sequel *Till I End My Song* - who spent his last years in Long Wittenham - is buried in the graveyard. Another erstwhile resident of renown and vision was Roye England the model maker and founder of the Pendon Museum who arrived here in 1954 and converted the old Three Poplars pub into a Youth Hostel.

Eating & Drinking

THE PLOUGH - High Street. Tel: 01867 207738. Homely village pub with a long garden leading down to the riverbank where there is good decking for mooring a couple of boats. Filling food and Greene King ales.

Shopping

Small post office stores adjacent to Pendon Museum, early closing Wed & Sat, closed Sun.

Things to Do

PENDON MUSEUM - 'museum' is a misnomer, Pendon houses an extraordinary 1:76 model of the Vale of the White Horse *c*1930s which has taken the best part of fifty years to build and work continues. Other exhibits include a railway running at the edge of Dartmoor and John Ahern's brilliant Madder Valley Railway. Spellbinding and absolutely not to be missed! Open 2-5pm Saturdays and Sundays and also Wednesdays in July and August. Tel: 01865 407365.

Connections

BUSES - Whites coaches run hourly between Dorchester and Didcot. Tel: 0870 608 2 608.

Sutton Courtenay (Map 24)

An embarrassment of fine buildings characterises this quiet village on ostensibly un-navigable backwaters. Unfortunately it is some distance on foot from the nearest moorings on Culham Reach. A mere detail, which should not dissuade you from visiting Sutton, the pools are utterly picturesque and Eric Blair (aka George Orwell) is buried towards the bottom right corner of the churchyard which also includes the grave of the Liberal P.M. Asquith. There are three fine pubs, notably THE FISH, a Les Routiers recommended inn noted for its seafood menu. Tel: 01235 848242.

Dorchester (Map 25)

Not to be confused with Thomas Hardy's Dorchester, Dorchester-on-Thames (and surely that should be Dorchester-on-*Thame* !) is a gloriously sleepy place, by-passed (relatively recently) by the main road and by-passed, it appears, by time itself. O-level historians will realise, given the second syllable of its name, that it boasts Roman origins. Accessible from moorings above or below Day's Lock - from which a footpath leads across the prehistoric mounds of the Dyke Hills - the centre is dominated by a Decorated Abbey approached through a Butterfield lych gate and justly renowned for its astonishing Jesse window. Picturesque, and tiny by comparison, the Catholic church is also worth a peep.

Eating & Drinking

THE GEORGE HOTEL - High Street. This three star hotel was originally a coaching inn and can trace its history back to the 15th century. Tel: 01865 340404.

THE WHITE HART - High Street. Ditto above. Tel: 01865 340074. Recently refurbished and recommended by the *Good Beer Guide*.

FLEUR DE LYS - High Street. 16th century pub. Tel: 01865 340502. Bed & Breakfast. *Tea Room annex to the Abbey also.*

Shopping

Well known as a centre for antiques, Dorchester's practical shopping is restricted to a small Co-op store and a post office.

Things to Do

ABBEY MUSEUM - Tel: 01865 340751. Small museum devoted to local history and the abbey. Open May-September, Tuesday-Saturday 11am-5pm and Sundays 2pm-5pm.

Connections

BUSES - Thames Travel Service 138 links Dorchester with Wallingford and Abingdon. Tel: 0870 608 2 608.

N some circles - albeit ever decreasing ones - the Thames above its confluence with the confusingly named Thame is known as Isis. This River Thame, navigable as far as Dorchester by the intrepid crews of diminutive vessels, rises to the east of Aylesbury, close to the Grand Union Canal. Its name derives from an eponymous market town on the north-eastern border of Oxfordshire notable in that the eccentric restaurateur John Fothergill once kept the Spread Eagle there. John Masefield (*Sea Fever*, *The Box of Delights*) lived beside the river at Burcot for many years. Hereabouts the Thames is dominated visually hereabouts by the Sinodun Hills, alias Wittenham Clumps; little more than three hundred feet above sea level, though positively mountainous in the context of the Thames flood plain. The artist Paul Nash was captivated by these scenes, especially under moonlight, and produced

make it your business to explore Little Wittenham Nature Reserve, lovingly tended by the Northmoor Trust. Waymarked trails lead through the woods or to the top of Round Hill and Castle Hill from which there are prodigious views and remnants of Iron Age fortifications. From these superior viewpoints more visual sense can be made of the Dyke Hills on the east bank of the river above Day's Lock, another example of ancient defences.

Shillingford Bridge, graceful, dating from 1827 and marking the halfway point between Reading and Oxford, is overlooked by an hotel with a riverside open air swimming pool. The Irish poet Yeats lived briefly in Shillingford during 1921.

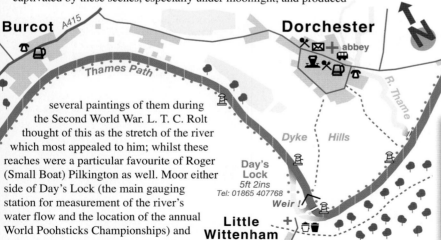

several paintings of them during the Second World War. L. T. C. Rolt thought of this as the stretch of the river which most appealed to him; whilst these reaches were a particular favourite of Roger (Small Boat) Pilkington as well. Moor either side of Day's Lock (the main gauging station for measurement of the river's water flow and the location of the annual World Poohsticks Championships) and

Day's Lock 5ft 2ins Tel: 01865 407768

Weir !

Shillingford

The wharf here used to serve a long gone brewery and goods were discharged for the larger village of Warborough to the north. Now all is peace. Look out for the flood level markings on an adjacent wall and be thankful you weren't hereabouts on the 27th January 1809 !

SHILLINGFORD BRIDGE HOTEL - riverside. Customer moorings. Tel: 01865 858657. Comfortable three star hotel offering bar and restaurant food to non residents.

Romance on Clifton Cut

Benson Lock

Clifton Hampden Bridge

Keeper's Cottage
Day's Lock

53

THE Thames moves at a more sedate pace than its 21st century hinterland. Journeying on or beside it offers the opportunity to fall back through the years to what we now perceive as a gentler era of canvassed camping skiffs and meadowland picnics. Solely a proliferation of abandoned pill boxes introduces a sense of unease. You wonder what were they designed to protect, and the answer is RAF Benson, closely associated with de Havilland 'Mosquitos'. In the Second World War these aircraft had sufficient range to reach the Balkans, and Benson was home of the Photographic Reconnaissance Unit. Nowadays it remains a vibrant base for Merlin and Puma helicopters. Benson Lock cottage is dated 1913, before the concept of world wars existed at all. Flood level plaques adorn its walls, some suspiciously pre-dating it! The Thames Path changes banks, and the walker enjoys an entertaining interlude bridging the lengthy weir. Jethro Tull - the inventor of the horse-drawn seed drill, not the 1960s rock band - lived in Crowmarsh Gifford between 1700 and 1710 - see also Map 28.

Wallingford Bridge boasts seventeen arches, though only five span the river. There is a charge for mooring overnight upstream on the town side of this bridge - downstream the far bank is gratis and the preserve of the *hoi polloi*. Not that one begrudges payment for so lovely a setting. The bridge is overlooked by the slender open spire of St Peter's Church, and a converted warehouse recalls the days when Wallingford relied more fully on the river for its commerce than it does now. Altogether a pleasingly mellow scene, marred only by the garish umbrellas flaunted by the neighbouring beer house. Interestingly, the town council consider £5 for vessels of less than 35 feet and £8 for anything over a reasonable price to pay, though it is significant that upstream at Abingdon the municipal moorings come free of charge.

Though their attitude to boaters differs, Wallingford and Abingdon

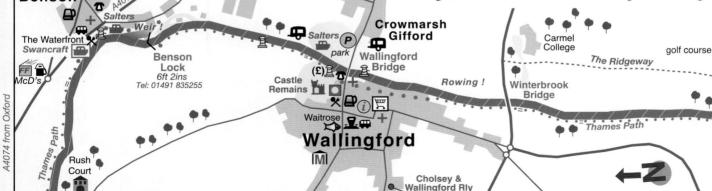

A4130 to Didcot   A329 to Reading

were firmly against the advent of the Railway Age, both spurning Brunelian advances to bring the Great Western Railway to their doorstep. The entrenched self-interest of river traders may have had a bearing on this hostility, but it did result in isolation from the march of 19th century commerce and industry. Eventually both towns lowered their guard and linked themselves umbilically to the main line, but too late for their shortlived branches - closed to passengers respectively in 1959 and 1963

- to rouse their towns out of their historic torpor.

South of Winterbrook Bridge, which carries Wallingford by-pass across the Thames, the Thames Path is joined by The Ridgeway, the two National Trails hugging their respective riverbanks as far as Streatley. The Ridgeway runs from Avebury in Wiltshire to Ivinghoe Beacon in Hertfordshire, a distance of eighty-five miles. Carmel College is a Jewish independent school.

Benson (Map 26)

Also occasionally known as Bensington, Benson is chiefly known for its RAF base these days, though a couple of centuries ago it was an important staging post for coaches on the Oxford to Henley run. The centre of the village lies across the busy A4074.

Eating & Drinking

THE WATERFRONT - versatile and egalitarian riverside cafe/restaurant. Tel: 01491 833732. *There is also a pub in the village.*

Shopping

Newspapers, gifts and limited groceries available from a shop adjunct to the cafe. Otherwise you'll have to walk into the village centre (taking care of the traffic) where you'll find a small Somerfield supermarket, butcher, grocer, pharmacy, off licence, post office and newsagent.

Connections

BUSES - Thames Travel service 105 runs hourly to/from Oxford, Dorchester, Wallingford and Cholsey. Tel: 0870 608 2 608.

Wallingford (Map 26)

The prehistoric origins of 'Walling Ford' are self explanatory. Alfred the Great fortified the town against the Danes and William the Conqueror erected a castle here. It dominated the town for five hundred years and in the 12th century supported Queen Matilda against King Stephen. When decay set in, Henry VIII ordered much of its timber and lead to be shipped downstream for enlarging Windsor Castle. Nowadays Wallingford wears such history lightly and is fun to perambulate. Work outwards from the Tourist Information Centre housed in the old Town Hall and you won't go far wrong.

Eating & Drinking

THE BOATHOUSE - riverside by Wallingford Bridge. Big screen bar & grill. Tel: 01491 834200. WALLINGFORD TANDOORI - High Street (adjacent river bridge). Tel: 01491 836249. AVANTI - High Street. Stylish Italian restaurant. Tel: 01491 835500. SAN SICARIO - High Street. Ditto but less expensive and livelier. Tel: 01491 834078. GEORGE HOTEL - High Street. Tel: 01491 836665. Bar & restaurant meals in a nicely appointed hotel. THE DOLPHIN - St Mary's Street. Nice little town pub, food and accommodation. Greene King beers and homemade pies. Tel: 01491 837377.

Shopping

Wallingford is a pleasant place to shop in with a WAITROSE supermarket well-integrated into the centre of town and a revelation for northern types brought up on ASDA and Morrisons. DOWN TO EARTH on St Martins Street (adjacent the lovely parish church with its wildlife churchyard) deals in local produce, freshly baked bread and homemade cakes. TOBY ENGLISH'S secondhand bookshop on St Mary's Street usually has an excellent selection of Thames related material. Friday is market day and there's a launderette on High Street within easy reach of the river.

Things to Do

TOURIST INFORMATION - Market Sq. Tel: 01491 826972. WALLINGFORD MUSEUM - High Street. Tel: 01491 835065. Open Mar-Nov, Tue-Fri afternoons, Saturdays 10.30-5pm. Also Sundays Jun & Aug. CHOLSEY & WALLINGFORD RAILWAY - Tel: 01491 835067. Short preserved train rides on 'The Bunk'.

Connections

BUSES - from the Market Square buses make frequent connections with Oxford and Reading and the nearest railheads at Cholsey and Didcot Parkway. Tel: 0870 608 2 608. TAXIS - Zodiac. Tel: 01491 201747.

EVER a dull moment as the Thames flows purposefully through the Goring Gap, an Ice Age leftover between the Berkshire Downs and The Chilterns. Walkers have to decide which pathway suits them best: the Thames Path upstream of Streatley hugging the west bank, The Ridgeway the east. Sadly the old ferries at Little Stoke and Moulsford no longer function, so crossing the river and combining the paths into circular walks is not a ready option. Moulsford Railway Bridge was originally the work of Isambard Kingdom Brunel and as such dates from 1840. When the line was quadrupled fifty years later, a second span was added on the downstream side, linked to the older bridge by curious little cross arches.

Moulsford ferry was immortalised anonymously by H. G. Wells in his delightful novel *The History of Mr. Polly*, which, by virtue of the chapter called 'The Potwell Inn' alone, deserves its niche in the pantheon of Thames inspired literature. Apparently Wells stayed at the Beetle & Wedge Inn whilst engaged on the book. Alfred Polly, who found convivial employment as the ferryman, would not recognise the inn now, for it has become smart and orientated in the general direction of fine cuisine, but his memory lingers affectionately on in the minds of ferry enthusiasts.

Cleeve Lock, the shallowest on the Thames, is backed by a maze of islets and backwaters, in one of which a maintenance yard tries manfully to disguise its utilitarian purpose. The pound between the locks at Goring and Cleeve is the shortest on the river, whilst, strangely, that between Cleeve and Benson is the lengthiest. Goring Bridge carries both The Ridgeway and the Thames Path across the river, its length necessitated by the weir channel and the millstream, a quintessential Thames scene of great charm. Oscar Wilde once lived in the old Ferry Cottage which later became the home of 'Bomber Harris', the controversial architect of Britain's blanket bombing raids on Germany.

26

North Stoke

The Ridgeway

Thames Path

Psychiatric Hospital

Papist Way

site of ferry

Little Stoke Manor

Oxon

Moulsford Railway Bridge

Keep to Channel !

Morning Star

DIDCOT

Offlands Farm

Thames Path

school

Sheridan Marine

site of ferry

South Stoke

Perch & Pike

Beetle & Wedge

Moulsford

B4009

Leatherne Bottel

Weir !

Sailing !

Berkshire

(£) Cleeve Lock
2ft 3ins
Tel: 01491 872608 (£)

Thames Path

Goring Lock
5ft 10ins
Tel: 01491 872687

The Swan

Weir !

site of ferry

A329

A417 to Wantage

B4009 to Newbury

READING

Goring

Miller of Mansfield

WC

Catherine Wheel

John Barleycorn

Goring Bridge

Thames Path

28

YHA The Bull

Streatley

Goring (Map 27)

Perhaps the quintessential Thameside village, Goring has been the scene of an annual regatta since 1887. Good moorings below the bridge offer easy access to quaint streets where the use of flint and timber is prevalent. The Norman church boasts one of the oldest bells in Britain. Walkers on The Ridgeway and Thames Path may doff their hats to each other as they cross the river.

Eating & Drinking

MELA - Bridge Approach. Tel: 01491 872243. Bangladeshi restaurant and take-away handy for the moorings.
THE MILLER OF MANSFIELD - High Street. Tel: 01491 872829. Bar and restaurant meals.
CATHERINE WHEEL - Station Road. Homely little local. Tel: 01491 872379.
MASOOM'S - High Street. Tandoori restaurant & take-away. Tel: 01491 872796.
JOHN BARLEYCORN - Manor Road. Tel: 01491 872509. Brakspear ales, food & accommodation.
LITTLE JOLLY GOOD FOOD CO - High Street. Petite cafe sibling to the brasserie in Pangbourne.
LEATHERNE BOTTEL - Cleeve. Tel: 01491 872667. Smart restaurant in gorgeous riverside setting upstream of Cleeve Lock. Conde Nast Johansens 'Most Excellent Restaurant' 2006.

Shopping

Sad to relate, Napper's old-fashioned grocery store has bit the dust, but Goring remains a good spot to lay on stores without having to fight your way through the crowds. Facilities include two banks, a post office (beside the bridge), convenience store, butcher, off licence, pharmacist, gift shop, gallery and a dealer in toys and teddy bears. A small back room in BARBARA'S ANTIQUES does a nice line in

Goring Bridge

Thames literature and GWR books and ephemera.

Connections

TRAINS - First Great Western stopping services to/from London, Reading and Oxford. Tel: 08457 484950.
BUSES - Thames Travel service 132 links Goring with Benson and Reading via Wallingford and many other river villages. Tel: 0870 608 2 608.

Streatley (Map 27)

Odd how each river crossing throws up neighbouring communities where the economy of one has thrived at the expense of the others. In this case Streatley is the shy, retiring type and many would remark all the more appealing for it, and indeed there are some charming brick buildings in the vernacular Thames Valley style.

Eating & Drinking

THE SWAN - highly regarded riverside hotel open to non-residents. Beautiful waterside gardens with an Oxford College barge permanently moored alongside. Tel: 01491 873737. Al fresco meals in summer.
THE BULL - Reading Road. Nice old pub at the top of the village. Food & families welcome. Tel: 01491 872507.

South Stoke (Map 27)

Idyllic village isolated from the outside world by the river and the railway. The 13th century church notable for its glass. Other buildings use tile, thatch, flint and weatherboarding to much effect. Suitable moorings by the old ferry staithe.

Eating & Drinking

PERCH & PIKE - village centre. Tel: 01491 872415. Really lovely Les Routiers recommended village pub offering food and accommodation.

Moulsford (Map 27)

A corruption of 'Mules Ford'. The church is the work of George Gilbert Scott and lies hidden between the road and the riverbank. The inn gets its name from tools used in wood cutting; a 'beetle' being a heavy type of mallet. As well as being associated with H.G. Wells, another literary guest was George Bernard Shaw.

Eating & Drinking

BEETLE & WEDGE HOTEL - Ferry Lane. Tel: 01491 651381. Sophisticated eating establishment offering a choice of restaurants.

Cholsey (Map 27)

The Great War poet, Edward Thomas, crossed the Thames by ferry from Little Stoke to Cholsey and walked up the Papist Way while researching on foot his book *The Icknield Way*. In the bar of the Morning Star he eavesdropped as a drayman and a butcher's boy agreed that motor-cars were ruining the roads. What prescience, for this was 1912! Agatha Christie is buried in the isolated churchyard beyond the railway.

FORMING the boundary between Berkshire and Oxfordshire, the river makes attractive progress through a gracious landscape full of historical and natural interest. In the churchyard at Lower Basildon Jethro Tull, previously encountered at Crowmarsh Gifford on Map 26, is buried. Beale Park wildlife centre is home to many rare breeds and endangered species and hosted the National Waterways Festival in 2006.

Briefly, the Thames Path detours away from the riverbank, though any disappointment incurred is amply compensated by being reunited with the river amidst the beech and yew tree and chalk cliff setting of Hartslock Wood, the name of which recalls the existence of a former lock in the neighbourhood.

It does not come as any great surprise to learn that Kenneth Grahame, who wrote the incomparable children's classic, *The Wind in the Willows*, spent a good deal of his life in Pangbourne and was inspired in telling the story to his young son by the river scenery of his own boyhood. You too will fall for the beauty of these reaches of the Thames and, like Mole, be 'intoxicated with the sparkle, the ripple, the scents and the sounds and the sunlight'.

On hot summer days Pangbourne's bravest dare each other to leap off Whitchurch Toll Bridge for a cool plunge in the Thames. The bridge is made of iron and was built in 1902. Sensibilities alter with time, for Eric de Mare, the photographer, architectural writer and close friend of L. T. C. Rolt proclaimed the bridge 'no beauty' in his book *Time on the Thames* published in 1952. Over fifty years later its whitewashed span gleams appealingly below the lock, and by modern standards looks anything but ugly, and it is the hard-hearted motorist who begrudges his twenty pence to cross such a characterful structure in such a gorgeous setting. Incidentally, the only other toll bridge on the Thames is at Swinford, some half dozen miles upstream of Oxford, which currently costs just five pence to negotiate, perhaps because the river is narrower! The tiny River Pang enters the Thames shyly, having risen on the Berkshire Downs south of Didcot. An alpaca herd grazes surreally on riverside pastures in the reach down to Mapledurham.

58

Pangbourne (Map 28)

A row of elegant late Victorian houses which line the riverbank to the west of Pangbourne are known as the 'Seven Deadly Sins'. Lady Cunard, the socialite, was once a resident here, and these houses set the rather racy tone for a likeable little town marred only by a surfeit of road traffic. Public moorings are to be found on the Berkshire bank downstream from Whitchurch Toll Bridge. To reach the centre on foot you must negotiate a constricted tunnel under the four track railway. Kenneth Grahame lived at Church Cottage and when he died the church was decorated with fresh willows in honour of his famous book.

Eating & Drinking

THE SWAN - riverbank, moorings for customers. Tel: 0118 984 4494. Famous old Thameside inn fondly remembered as the spot where the Three Men and Montmorency shamefacedly abandoned their boat and caught the train back to Paddington and the Alhambra. Bar and restaurant meals, families welcome.
MIA BENI - town centre. Italian restaurant just through the railway bridge. Tel: 0118 984 4440.
LINA TANDOORI - town centre. Likeable Indian restaurant and takeaway. Tel: 0118 984 5577.
LAUGHING HALIBUT - town centre. Fish & chips. Tel: 0118 984 1614.
JOLLY GOOD FOOD CO - Reading Road. Tel: 0118 984 2246. Licensed brasserie, great pies!

Shopping

A good collection of shops make Pangbourne a useful base. There are branches of the big four banks, a small Somerfield supermarket, and a branch of W. H. Smith. But it is the independents (as always) who catch the eye: THE SPINNEY delicatessen; GREENS butchers; and GREYS cheese and wine shop. A handy launderette for scutty boaters can be found near the station.

Things to Do

BEALE PARK - lovely wildlife sanctuary with moorings for visitors by boat. Miniature railway, adventure park, refreshments; deer, owls, goats, flamingos and lemurs. Tel: 0870 777 7160 www.bealepark.co.uk
BASILDON PARK - Tel: 0118 984 3040. 18th century Palladian mansion designed by John Carr (of York) for a man who made a fortune in India. Now operated by the National Trust and accessible from the west bank of the river at Lower Basildon.

Connections

TRAINS - frequent Thames Trains along the river corridor. Tel: 08457 484950.

Whitchurch-on-Thames (Map 28)

Peaceful and shopless, the picturesque houses of Whitchurch cling to a steep hill on the Oxfordshire bank of the Thames. Two pubs offer refreshment to walkers on the Thames Path: The Ferryboat (Tel: 0118 984 2161) and The Greyhound (Tel: 0118 984 2160).

Whitchurch Toll Bridge

DESPITE the proximity of the main line railway and the strung out suburbs of Tilehurst, the Thames retains its integrity, unimpeachably lovely however we care to compromise it. Reading is rapidly shaken off when travelling upstream, in the opposite direction it delays showing its urban hand until the last possible moment.

The Thames Path detours through the suburban environs of Purley, an incongruous excursion for serious walkers caused long ago by the obduracy of a local landowner who refused even the powerful Thames Commissioners access on to his meadowlands. As a result the towpath changed banks and two ferries plied back and forth with boat horses and pedestrians; naturally neither survive.

Rolling hills and woods characterise the view to the north. The environs of Mapledurham Lock - the first on the Thames to be mechanised in 1956 - are outstandingly scenic and a lockside tearoom (with plants for sale) adds to its popularity. Mapledurham House is of 16th century origin and is widely considered one of England's finest Tudor buildings. It was home to the Catholic Blounts, a secret tunnel leads to the adjoining church. Royalists used secret rooms and passages within the house during the Civil War. John Galsworthy wrote the final chapters of his *Forsyte Saga* whilst staying in the house and E. H. Shepard who illustrated *The Wind in the Willows*, is said to have been inspired by the setting. The adjoining watermill has been restored and is open to the public at set times. At one time its power was harnessed to provide the house with electricity.

Hardwick House is even older than Mapledurham. Elizabeth I stayed here and Kenneth Grahame is thought to have modelled Toad Hall on it.

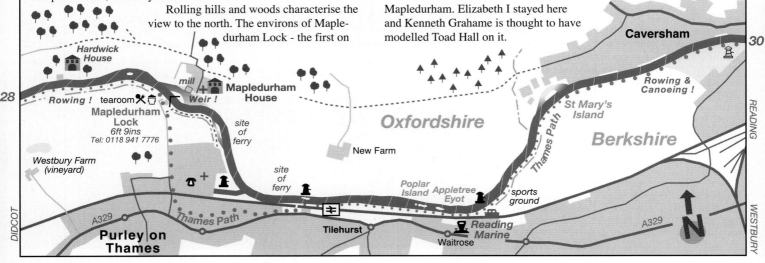

FOR such a large town, Reading lets its river off lightly, respecting its integrity and not allowing urbanisation to compromise matters. For once one does not necessarily find oneself in accord with Jerome K. Jerome's opinion that the river at Reading is 'dismal and dirty'. Caversham Bridge and Reading Bridge span the Thames as it skims the northern edge of the town. The present Caversham Bridge dates from 1926 and was (remarkably) one of three Thames bridges opened on exactly the same day by a busy Prince of Wales. In 1643 an earlier version of the bridge was the scene of a battle between the Earl of Essex and King Charles I during the Civil War. Downstream, Fry's Island plays host to two hire bases and a bowling club whose 'Bohemian' members have to make use of a private ferry to gain access to their neatly mown greens. Reading Bridge is three years older than its neighbour. When constructed it was one of the longest concrete spans then in existence. To prove that it was up to the job, a convoy of steam road-rollers was driven onto it to confirm its load-bearing qualities.

Caversham Lock lies in a bosky setting adjacent to parkland. Overlooked by gasholders, Kennet Mouth forms a misleadingly inauspicious beginning to the Kennet & Avon. On the opposite bank former gravel workings are enjoying a new lease of life recreationally as the Thames continues downstream towards Sonning.

*Figures refer to River Thames.

continued from page 42

Shopping

Bookended by Debenhams and the House of Fraser, THE ORACLE offers 21st century shopping, but you know our sympathies lie elsewhere. Come with us to Union Street (alias 'Smelly Alley') where FROSTS the fishmongers and DUDMANS the 'high class' greengrocers and GILBERTS the butchers ply their trade and you will have a clearer conscience. KEEGANS secondhand bookshop lurks on Merchants Place off Friar Street and is normally a good bet for railway and waterway literature. Farmers' Market on the first and third Saturdays of each month between 8.30am and 12pm. There are good moorings alongside a large TESCO supermarket on the Thames upstream of its confluence with the Kennet.

Things to Do

TOURIST INFORMATION - Church House, Chain Street. Tel: 0118 956 6226   www.readingtourism.org.uk
RIVERSIDE MUSEUM - Gasworks Road. Tel: 0118 939 9800. Reading's social and industrial history housed in a former sewage pumping station. Wonderfully elegant gypsy vado built on Kennetside circa 1914 takes pride of place.
MUSEUM OF READING - Town Hall. Tel: 0118 939 9800. Housed in Alfred Waterhouse's imposing town hall of 1875. Features a replica of the Bayeux Tapestry embroidered in Leek, Staffordshire in 1885.

Connections

TRAINS - services along the Thames and Kennet valleys. Tel: 08457 484950.
TAXIS - Royal Cars. Tel: 0118 956 0560.

HAKING off Reading's business parks, whilst skirting former gravel workings reinvented as rowing courses, the river runs down to Sonning (pronounced 'Sunning'), 'the most fairy-like little nook on the whole river' according to Jerome K. Jerome. One might argue with his first choice, whilst broadly agreeing with his sentiments; for, a century or so on, Sonning retains its fairy-tale atmosphere which one writer has likened to a Hollywood ideal of England. The brick-built lock house dates from the First World War. On the towpath side an iron gate decorated with oars commemorates a master from the adjoining Blue Coat School drowned in the vicinity on 26th January 1953.

Sonning Mill ceased grinding out a living in 1969, by which time it was the last on the Thames deriving power from its water-wheels. In its heyday it had operated a fleet of barges to bring wheat up from the Port of London and to convey milled flour to Huntley & Palmers biscuit factory at Reading. Happily, the mill enjoys a new lease of life as a restaurant and theatre. The picturesque bridge - of whose eleven arches solely the centre is navigable - dates from the 17th century, and on this strollers on the Thames Path must cross, exchanging Berks for Oxon or vice versa.

Downstream the river, lined by willows and reeds, threads low-lying pastures. The reach between Sonning and Shiplake feels unconvincingly remote, and briefly you are reminded of the Upper Thames between Oxford and Lechlade, but airliners, stacked up on the approach to Heathrow, quickly belie this enjoyable though false sense of seclusion.

Three islets precede Shiplake which sits perched on a chalky outcrop above the boathouses of Shiplake College whose pupils wear rather elegant, predominantly red blazers with blue and yellow stripes which would not look out of place were they to be provided by the wardrobe department in a filmed dramatization of *Three Men In A Boat* : fortunate young people to be educated in such surroundings.

Shiplake Lock is an idyllic spot, at its tail the modest River Loddon enters the Thames, followed by a bridge carrying the branch line railway which links the main line at Twyford with Henley.

Sonning (Map 31)

'Tinged with an Edwardian holiday, or musical-comedy, gaiety' wrote Betjeman & Piper in 1949 and you can still see where they were coming from; and money doesn't talk here so much as discreetly whisper. The Bishops of Salisbury had a palace near the imposing church, but perhaps the village's best building is Lutyens' Deanery Garden, built for the founder of *Country Life*. South of the Great West Road, Sonning Cutting is a two miles long, sixty foot deep gash engineered by Brunel (along with 1,220 navvies and 196 horses) in 1840 to effect the Great Western Railway's progress from London to Reading. Now mellowed by tree growth but once beloved of railway photographers.

Eating & Drinking

THE BULL - High Street. Tel: 0118 969 3901 Historic half-timbered inn recommended by Jerome K. Jerome in 1889, and time has not withered his opinion. Now owned by the Hampshire brewers Gale & Co who provide bar food, restaurant meals and accommodation to a high but not excessively expensive standard. GREAT HOUSE HOTEL - Thames Street (riverside). Tel: 0118 969 2277 www.greathouseatsonning.co.uk Ferryman's Bar and Regatta Restaurant. Customer moorings. THE MILL AT SONNING - Sonning Eye. Tel: 0118 969 8000 www.millatsonning.com Former 18th century flour mill (which retains a working water wheel) now imaginatively used as a Dinner Theatre where your meal is followed by a theatrical or musical performance - a lovely way to while away an afternoon or evening. Booking recommended. FRENCH HORN HOTEL - Sonning Eye. Tel: 0118 969 2204. Luxury hotel and gourmet restaurant with lawns sloping down to the backwater. Moorings for patrons sufficiently well-heeled.

Wargrave (Map 31)

Wargrave church was rebuilt in 1916 after suffering an arson attack by the Suffragettes. In the churchyard there is a mausoleum by Lutyens. On High Street look out for the art-nouveau styling of Woodclyffe Hall.

Eating & Drinking

ST GEORGE & DRAGON - riverside. Tel: 0118 940 5021. Smartly refurbished inn offering customer moorings for contemporary cooking. *Two more pubs in the village.*

Shopping

Solely a post office now it would seem.

Connections

TRAINS - halt on the 'Regatta Line' (see Henley), the four minute ride to Shiplake being a useful ruse by which pedestrians can effect a crossing of the river. Tel: 08457 484950.

Shiplake Lock

32 LOWER THAMES

THE absence of two ferries forces the Thames Path in a diversion away from the riverbank and through Lower Shiplake instead, bringing advantages and disadvantages to boaters and walkers in almost equal measure: the former miss the roadside entrances to some fine properties (one of which boasts a magnificent miniature railway complete with a scaled down version of a Germanic looking station building) the latter these selfsame properties' sublime river frontages. Hennerton Backwater can only realistically be navigated by small unpowered craft.

Between Ferry Eyot and Marsh Lock (and, indeed, all the way down to Henley) the riverbanks boast some remarkably handsome houses, many of which incorporate boathouses from which you can imagine teak launches emerging with elaborately costumed boating parties in the river's Victorian and Edwardian heyday. The Berkshire bank rises in a bluff of chalky cliff faces, and the A321 spans a lane running

down to the waterside on a rough-hewn bridge erected in the 18th century with stones garnered from the ruins of Reading Abbey. Intriguingly, this curious structure was built by the Rev. Humphrey Gainsborough, brother of the famous painter.

Attractive timber footbridges carry pedestrians over the backwaters and former millstreams either side of Marsh Lock. Once there were mills on either bank; one engaged in grinding flour the other a brass foundry. Humphrey Gainsborough is said to have been instrumental in construction of the first pound lock here in 1773.

Henley presents a welcoming face to river travellers. There are excellent mooring facilities (albeit with a fee payable overnight) either side of the handsome five arch bridge which dates from 1787.

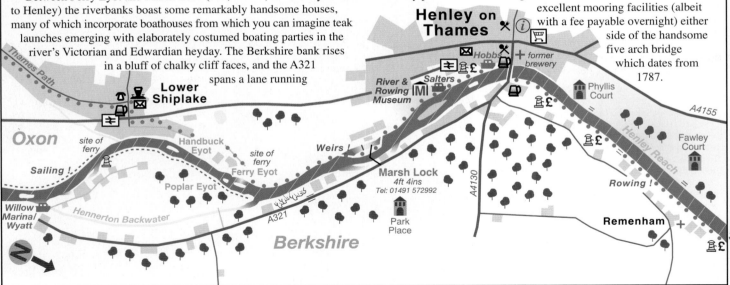

64

Newcomers, may experience a sense of deja vu, for Henley's waterfront is so iconic and so often represented on jigsaws, calendars and chocolate boxes that subconsciously it's only too easy to feel that you've somehow been here before. St Mary the Virgin's 16th Century church tower dominates the view - Dusty Springfield is buried in its churchyard.

But of course it is for the serious business of competitive rowing that Henley is world famous. The Regatta (held between the end of June and the beginning of July) dates back to 1839 and was conferred 'Royal' status in 1851. The Regatta course stretches from Temple Island to a point four hundred yards downstream of Henley Bridge. When it is in full flow, passing boaters are ushered through the 1 mile and 550 yards long course as expeditiously as possible, in full gaze of the well-dressed (and often well-oiled) throng: twelve thousand pints of Pimms; four and a half thousand bottles of champagne; and a ton of strawberries being consumed with gusto per annum. To those more versed in the utilitarian world of the canals, it is an experience not easily lived down.

The Regatta headquarters, opened by the Queen in 1986, stand alongside the town bridge on the Berkshire bank, cheek by jowl with the elaborate Edwardian premises of the Leander Rowing Club. Across the water two of Henley's most prestigious and historic hostelries, The Angel and The Red Lion, return their gaze with interest. Downstream on the Oxfordshire bank the tower and maltings of Brakspear's former brewery loom over the rooftops of riverside houses and then there are some ebullient Edwardian properties boasting balconies and boat houses which must have some racy stories to relate could mere bricks and mortar but talk.

The Thames Path elopes with the Berkshire bank downstream of Henley Bridge. Henley Reach is overlooked by Phyllis Court, a prestigious gentlemen's club and Fawley Court, the work of Sir Christopher Wren. Of more import to males of a certain age is the exciting truth that Jenny Agutter was married in Remenham church. Caled Gould, Hambleden's lock-keeper for almost sixty years, was buried in the churchyard in 1836.

Lower Shiplake (Map 32)

No easy access for boaters, but a useful stop on the Thames Path with pub, post office stores and railway station.

Henley on Thames (Map 32)

Outside the rush of Regatta week, Henley regresses, morphing back into its traditional role of a country market town, albeit a well-heeled example of the breed as exemplified by a profusion of eating places and upmarket emporiums. Mill Meadow with its grassy swards and ice cream parlours instils a seaside feel to the proceedings, even if overnight moorings come at a pricey £8.

Eating & Drinking

THE ANGEL ON THE BRIDGE - Thames Side. Tel: 01491 410678. Iconic pub offering bar and restaurant food with terrace overlooking the bridge. THE LITTLE ANGEL - Remenham Lane. Tel: 01491 411008. Smart refurbished pub across the river.

ANTICO - Market Place. Tel: 01491 573060. Authentic Italian.
HENLEY TEA ROOMS - Thameside. Tel: 01491 411412. Comfort food.
HOTEL DU VIN - New Street. Tel: 01491 848400. Bistro open to non-residents in original Brakspear brewery which once featured in an episode of *Inspector Morse*.
SPICE MERCHANT - Thameside. Tel: 01491 636118. Contemporary Indian overlooking the river. LOCH FYNE - Market Place. Tel: 01491 845780. Fish & seafood chain.

Shopping

A riverside JAEGER outlet sets the tone for some upmarket shopping opportunities, as exemplified by THE HEALTHY DELI on Duke Street - try their sumptuous Spanish Omelette. There are two good antiquarian booksellers - JONKERS on Hart Street, and WAY's on Friday Street - plus a good independent called THE BELL BOOKSHOP on Bell Street, where you'll also find WAITROSE. In the Market Place, GABRIEL MACHIN is an outstanding butcher's shop recommended by Rick Stein.

Things to Do

TOURIST INFORMATION - Tel: 01491 578034 *www.visit-henley.org.uk*
RIVER & ROWING MUSEUM - Mill Meadows. Tel: 01491 415600 *www.rrm.co.uk* Exceptionally well designed and interesting museum devoted to the River Thames, rowing, Henley itself and the *Wind in the Willows*. Excellent audio-visual aids, shop and cafe.

Connections

TRAINS - hourly First Greater Western shuttle (branded the 'Regatta line', a picturesque branchline which enjoyed its 150th anniversary in 2006) to/from Twyford with local connections thence to Reading or Paddington. Tel: 08457 484950.
BUSES - Arriva connect with Reading, Marlow and High Wycombe, Thames Travel with Wallingford. Tel: 0870 608 2 608.
TAXIS - Talbot. Tel: 01491 574222.

PUTTING Henley's famous rowing course behind it, the Thames progresses downstream past a sequence of fascinating houses, all with a history to tell. Temple Island originally belonged to the owners of Fawley Court. The 'temple' itself was designed as a fishing lodge in 1771 by James Wyatt. The river curves round to Hambledon Lock past the white stucco spread of Greenlands, now a business school, but originally the home of William Henry Smith, and amusingly described by the narrator of *Three Men In A Boat* as 'the residence of my newsagent', for the man in question was, of course, the founder of the retail chain W. H. Smith.

The river is wide hereabouts and backed by stately wooded hills to the north. Hambleden Lock is overlooked by a picturesque weatherboarded mill, long since converted from the real business of corn milling into expensive accommodation. A mile north of Mill End lies the quintessentially English village of Hambleden, used for filming by the makers off *The Midsomer Murders*.

The demise of Aston Ferry again forces the Thames Path away from the riverbank, but by way of consolation the detour offers walkers the opportunity of refreshment at the Flower Pot Hotel, an unspoilt inn

still charmingly advertising that it provides 'good accommodation for fishing and boating parties'. Walkers are also treated to a close-up view of Culham Court and its impressive topiary. George III was a guest here once and warm rolls wrapped in hot flannel by his favourite baker in London were rushed down to the pampered king by horse relay.

Medmenham Abbey bore witness to the debauched orgies of the infamous Hellfire Club in the middle of the 18th century, but the history of the site goes back much further to the establishment of a Cistercian foundation whose monks were allegedly much better behaved. Danesfield (built for a man who made his fortune in soap) looks disdainfully down across the river to a static caravan park; there could hardly be a greater contrast in the provision of accommodation for the same species. An archipelago of wooded islands add mystery and atmosphere to the backwaters of Hurley Lock. Glimpsed amidst the trees, Harleyford Manor is one of several grand Thames-side houses said to have been the inspiration for Toad Hall!

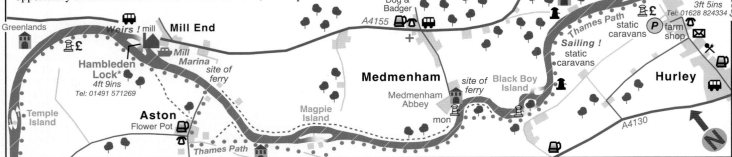

Medmenham (Map 33)

Now that the Hellfire orgies have abated, this is a peaceful spot and it appears possible to moor upstream of the conspicuous monument which commemorates a successful legal action brought in 1899 by Viscount Devonport to confirm the ferry's public, as opposed to private, status; a hollow victory, for the boat ceased plying between the wars.

Eating & Drinking
DOG & BADGER - on A4155 approximately half a mile from the river. Tel: 01491 571362.

Connections
BUSES - Arriva services 328/9 connect with Henley and Marlow. Tel: 0870 608 2 608.

TAXIS - see Henley or Marlow.

Aston (Map 33)

Eating & Drinking
THE FLOWER POT - Tel: 01491 574721. Idyllic pub in the image of 'The Potwell Inn'. Decidedly free range poultry roam the beer garden. Rough moorings by the site of the ferry or walk back from above Hambleden Lock.

Hurley (Map 33)

Trance-like village which once boasted a Benedictine Priory, but now plays host to a static caravan park.

Eating & Drinking
YE OLDE BELL - village centre. Tel: 01628 825881. Half-timbered, flower bedecked Ramada Jarvis hotel with gorgeous garden.

RISING SUN - village centre. Tel: 01628 824274. Modest neighbour!

Shopping
Farm shop (Tel: 01628 824271) and post office stores.

Connections
BUSES - Courtney Coaches operate four times a day Mon-Sat to/from Henley and Maidenhead. Tel: 0870 608 2 608.

TAXIS - see Henley or Marlow

Hambleden Lock

67

THE pound between Hurley and Temple locks is the second shortest on the Thames. Temple Footbridge was erected in 1989 to replace a ferry abandoned over forty years earlier. New housing occupies the site of a former foundry which once received copper by boat from South Wales via the Thames & Severn Canal. A rock located beside the towpath commemorates Giles Every, a local rowing enthusiast who was killed in a motoring accident in 1984.

Have your autograph book at the ready when passing Bisham Abbey, for this is where the English football team come to train, all a far cry from the days when it was presented to Anne of Cleves by Henry VIII by way of consolation for his decision to divorce her: Queen Elizabeth I is said to have spent some of her childhood here. Bisham's picturesque parish church also adorns the Berkshire bank, being feted for its Hoby chapel and monuments.

Marlow lies roughly half way between Oxford and London. The suspension bridge which spans the river at Marlow dates from 1832 and is the work of an engineer called William Tierney Clark. He later went on to design a larger

suspension bridge linking Buda on one bank of the Danube with Pest on the other. In Eric de Mare's opinion the structure is a good example of 'that period when engineering and architecture enjoyed a brief but happy marriage' and 'forms an excellent foil to the spire' of All Saints Church, an exact contemporary. Perhaps the best view of these mutually inclusive but unlikely bedfellows is upstream from Marlow Lock, employing the natural perspective of the curving weir to draw the eye towards both church and bridge. This is one of the Thames' most definitive scenes, and the sole disappointment lies in the niggling absence now of Marlow Mill which used to make flour from locally produced grain and paper from rags brought upstream from London by barge. Sadly, in the Philistine Sixties, the millstream was dammed, the mill demolished, and flats erected in a half-hearted parody of vernacular styling in its place.

Downstream from Marlow Lock the river passes beneath the town's noisy by-pass but quickly finds balm as it skirts the wooded slopes of Quarry Wood, said to have been the

By-roads to Cookham Dean

68

inspiration for Kenneth Grahame's Wild Wood. Neighbouring Winter Hill is terraced by spectacular houses whose views, one imagines, can only be classified sublime. On the Berkshire side rugby pitches are separated from the water's edge by a narrow belt of woodland with benches and picnic tables. Marlow's branch line railway shadows the river's progress. Once this was the lair of the 'Marlow Donkey', a diminutive push & pull train which spent its life plying to and from Bourne End, where connections were made with the trains which formerly linked High Wycombe with Maidenhead. In 1970 a cheeseparing bout of rationalisation (one might better term it *ir*rationalisation) saw the line being abandoned between Bourne End and High Wycombe and services confined to a shuttle operation between Marlow and Maidenhead involving reversal at Bourne End. Still, it's good to see the little diesel trains trundling through these Thameside pastures, as innocent a form of landbased transport as one could hope for.

Marlow   (Map 34)

The configuration of park, church and river bridge smacks of Henley, but Marlow is far more demure. Like Henley, however - and, for that matter Abingdon as well - Marlow is a town whose brewery, once a major employer, has closed down; in this case it was Wethered's who fell prey to Whitbread and closed in 1988. You cannot, though, fail to progess far up the High Street without encountering the brewery's husk, an ache for those mindful of regionality, however amenably converted into housing and offices. A series of statues and plaques recall some of Marlow's famous sons and daughters: an impressario who foundered with the *Lusitania* in 1915; Edward John Gregory, the painter of Boulter's Lock (Map 35); T. S. Eliot; Edwin Clark the Victorian engineer; Thomas Love Peacock the novelist and his friends the Shelleys, of whom Mary is said to have written *Frankenstein* here.

Eating & Drinking

BURGERS - The Causeway. Tel: 01628 483389 *www.burgersofmarlow.co.uk* Swiss owned tearoom, craft baker and chocolatier. Breakfasts, omelettes and Swiss Rarebit!
PENGUIN FISH BAR - West Street. Tel: 01628 477271. Eat in or take-away fish & chips.
THE VANILLA POD - West Street. Tel: 01628 898101 *www.thevanillapod.co.uk* Fine dining in

Bisham

building where T. S. Eliot once lived. Not Suns.
PACHANGA - West Street. Tel: 01628 486000. Reputedly excellent Mexican restaurant.
THE MARLOW DONKEY - Station Road. Tel: 01628 482022. Refurbished Greene King pub recalling the name of the local push & pull train.
VILLA D'ESTE - Chapel Street. Tel: 01628 472012. Charming Italian.
ZIZZI'S - High Street. Tel: 01628 890200. Contemporary Italian chain housed in part of old brewery.
THE COMPLEAT ANGLER - Marlow Bridge. Tel: 01628 484444 *www.compleatangler-hotel.co.uk* Inspired by Izaak Walton, classy hotel with restaurant, brasserie and bars open to non-residents.

Shopping

It is probably no longer feasible to effect a triumphant exit from provisioning here in the manner of Jerome K. Jerome, George, Harris and Montmorency along with a cortege of shop boys, but nowadays Marlow lacks nothing in the Thames Valley's recurring theme of sophisticated shopping; though Waitrose are causing a rumpus over plans to build a huge new store. The Farmers & Food Market on the first Wednesday in the month on The Causeway (by the river bridge) sounds fun, but note that they up sticks at one thirty. HORIZONS is a good independent bookshop at the top of the High Street.

Things to Do

TOURIST INFORMATION - High Street. Tel: 01628 483597.

Connections

TRAINS - First Great Western links with Bourne End, Cookham and Maidenhead. Tel: 08457 484950.
BUSES - Arriva services 328/9 link Marlow with Henley and High Wycombe. Tel: 0870 608 2 608.
TAXIS - A1. Tel: 01628 851477.
CYCLE HIRE - SADDLE SAFARI, Crown Lane. Tel: 01628 477020.

ART, politics and wealth are the sub-texts of this section of the Thames, and for many these reaches mark the river's apotheosis. The delightful premises of the Upper Thames Sailing Club set the tone for Bourne End, a jaunty riverside village. The Thames Path crosses sides by way of a footbridge cantilevered out from the railway bridge in recent years to remedy a conspicuous absence of ferries, of which no fewer than four have perished. Cock Marsh is a Site of Special Scientific Interest, a throwback landscape somehow inured from the pressures of Thames Valley expansionism. Backed by a furzy escarpment, the Berkshire bank contrasts markedly with the residental glamour of the Buckinghamshire side of the river.

Cookham Reach is another prone to dinghy manoeuvres, but it leads expansively down to Stanley Spencer's former abode, revelling in scenes which inspired one of the greatest, not to say idiosyncratic, of 20th Century painters who was in the habit of wheeling his painting materials around the neighbourhood in a pram. Cookham Bridge is a Victorian structure of cast iron construction, made by a foundry as far away as Darlington!

These days it is painted a garish blue, but in Spencer's painting *Swan Upping at Cookham* it appears more modestly in brown and green. Three missing ferries force the Thames Path away from the riverbank in the vicinity of Cookham, and this is a great shame because the lock cut is especially lovely - even by the high standards of the Thames - a popular resort where refreshments are available from a lockside kiosk.

'You can't walk by the river at Cliveden Reach and not believe in God' was Stanley Spencer's firm belief, but the environs had an altogether different impact on John Profumo when he was a guest of Viscount Astor at Cliveden in July 1961; encountering not a deity but a naked nemesis in a swimming pool. Her name was Christine Keeler, and the rest, as they say, is well-documented history. But this chance meeting hastened the demise of an hitherto imperious Conservative government and, along with the Lady Chatterley case and the Beatles' first LP, a purblind age of post-war innocence.

Cliveden can trace its origins back to the 17th Century. In 1668 the Duke of Buckingham killed the Earl of Shrewsbury in a duel on the terrace. *Rule Britannia* was first performed here at a masque in 1740, under the baton of Thomas Arne, its composer. Three disastrous fires spelt an end to its earlier manifestations, and the present mansion, designed by Charles Barry for the Duke of Sutherland, dates from 1851. It belongs to the National Trust who sub-let it as an hotel. It enjoyed a heyday under the ownership of the wealthy Astor family and gained a dubious reputation in the mid 1930s when the 'Cliveden Set' of movers and shakers propagated appeasement with Nazi Germany. Look back on it from Bavin's Gulls to see it at its vainglorious best. A trio of Arts & Crafts style cottages overlook the river, the furthest downstream being Spring Cottage, built for the Duchess of Sutherland in 1857 by George Devey for use as a summer house. This is where Christine Keeler was staying as a guest of Stephen Ward before the Profumo scandal broke. In earlier days the Duchess would entertain Queen Victoria to tea in the secluded garden. Nowadays it's available for exclusive holiday lets through the hotel. In the adjoining boat house a flotilla of vintage launches is maintained for the amusement of Cliveden guests. Turner's *Barge on the River, Sunset*, painted in 1805, illustrates bargemen mooring for the night on Cliveden Reach. Boulter's Lock was made famous by E. J. Gregory's 1898 painting depicting it thronged with with pleasure craft on a *fin de siecle* Sunday afternoon presided over by the redoutable lock-keeper W. H. Turner and his faithful hound Juggins. For those already familiar with Gregory's ebullient picture, reality is something of a let down, as the modern day lock setting is compromised by a suburban road and the gaudy canopies of an ice cream kiosk.

Cliveden Reach

Bourne End (Map 35)

Behind the riverbank's pretty facade, Edwardian villas give way to suburbia, and the jauntiness subsides.

Eating & Drinking

THE BOUNTY - riverside upstream of rail bridge. Tel: 01628 520056. Homely and welcoming pub self-billed as the People's Republic of Cockmarsh. Sixty metres of quality mooring decking for patrons.
OTT - Bourne End Marina. Tel: 01628 523111. Upper storey restaurant overlooking marina and moorings.
INDIA GARDEN - The Parade. Tel: 01628 523212. Contemporary Indian restaurant offering take-away option.
SUPER PLAICE - The Parade. Tel: 01628 521968. Fish & chips.
SPADE OAK - Coldmoorholme Lane (Map 34). Tel: 01628 520090. Brewers Fayre pub/restaurant at the end of a quiet cul de sac and reached via a railway crossing from good moorings upstream of Bourne End.

Shopping

Suburban shopping featuring a pharmacy, butcher, grocery, newsagent/post office, off-licence, bakery, and NatWest bank. Small Somerfield and Co-op supermarkets.

Connections

TRAINS - First Great Western branchline services to/from Marlow and Maidenhead. Tel: 08457 484950.

Cookham (Map 35)

Cookham dwells rather smugly on its riverbank and Stanley Spencer lies in its churchyard, doubtless ruminating on the unforgiving march of property values, and the misplacement of other more important values. Cookham Moor is a wide open landscape looked after by the National Trust.

Eating & Drinking

THE FERRY - riverside. Tel: 01628 525123. Refurbished riverside inn belonging to the same group as the St George & Dragon at Wargrave - Map 31. Well-appointed, classy menu, nice waterside terrace, limited customer moorings.
BEL & THE DRAGON - High Street. Tel: 01628 521263. Comfortable pub with cosy interior and 'contemporary' garden for al fresco eating. Sophisticated bar and restaurant food, Fullers and Brakspear ales.

Cliveden

PEKING INN - High Street. Tel: 01628 520900. Chinese restaurant.
MALIK'S - High Street. Tel: 01628 520085. Tandoori.

Shopping

Cookham is bereft of food shops, though there are plenty of ladies fashion shops and beauty parlours. While their womenfolk are so engaged, mere males can patronize a fine wine merchant, a model railway shop and a fishing outlet.

Things to Do

SPENCER GALLERY - High Street. Tel: 01628 471885 www.stanleyspencer.org.uk Former Methodist Chapel converted as a shrine to this most parochial yet talented of 20th Century English painters who was born at the house called Fernlea on High Street in 1891. Pride of place goes to his radiant vision of *Christ Preaching at Cookham Regatta,* unfinished at his death in 1959.
CLIVEDEN - access for boaters via National Trust moorings on Cliveden Reach which are idyllic, if informal, and there is an overnight charge of £6. Tel: 01628 605069. 'Camelot-on-Thames' is how Nancy Astor was wont to describe Cliveden, Charles Barry's ostentatiously Italianate mansion built for the Duke of Sutherland in 1851. The house itself, now a luxurious hotel - Tel: 01628 668561 www.clivedenhouse.co.uk - is only partially open to the public under the auspices of the National Trust on a couple of afternoons per week, but the enchanting grounds more than make up for this, both in the formal gardens and the woodland walks. The former Ferry Cottage and its neighbour, New Cottage, are available for holiday lets from the NT - Tel: 0870 458 4422.

Connections

TRAINS - as per Bourne End. The station is located at Cookham Rise approximately half a mile to the west.

FLOWING North to South, the Thames skims Maidenhead and finds itself spanned by three great trade routes: the old Great West Road, the Great Western Railway, and the M4 Motorway. The gracious lines of Maidenhead Bridge date from 1772. It is the work of one Sir Robert Taylor, and if you mentally filter out the dross of its 21st Century surroundings, you can't help but picture stage coaches trundling over it, Bath bound in the age of Beau Brummell. Skindles Hotel, empty and boarded-up now on the Buckinghamshire bank of the river, is a ghostly, derisive echo of its rollicking past.

It is a generality that successive bridges lack the panache of their predecessors, and suffer by comparison. At Maidenhead, however, Brunel's railway bridge - Taylor's junior by sixty-seven years - wins all the plaudits, not least in its status as the flattest and widest brick arch in the world. As it was being built, lesser men than Brunel predicted its collapse with confidence. Some aural response to the ellipticity of the arches creates a spectacular echo which you may like to try out.

Between Maidenhead and Bray the Berkshire bank of the river plays host to many sumptuous houses, though some illustrate a greater awareness of the value of wealth than good taste. Some of the older,

more demure properties hark back to the *fin de siecle* days of the 19th Century when it became something of a vogue for society mothers to summer their daughters here in the hope that they might attract the attention of officers from the nearby Brigade of Guards club.

Bray Lock leads to Dorney Reach. The M4 spans the river on a bridge dating from 1961 which makes no attempt to emulate the aestheticism of either of the bridges at Maidenhead. Monkey Island is home to a wedding cake confection of an hotel housed in a building built in 1738 by the Duke of Marlborough for use as a fishing lodge. Oakley Court is also a hotel nowadays, its origins date back to the middle of the 19th Century when it was erected by a man who wished to cure his French wife of homesickness. In the nineteen-fifties it was used for making horror movies! Two busy marinas add to boat traffic on this reach, which perhaps explains why Eton College elected to create a purpose-built rowing course from former gravel workings.

Bray
Smug gastronomic cornucopia famous for its 17th Century vicar and his weathercock attitude to politics and religion. Hosts now the WATERSIDE INN (Tel: 01628 620691) Roux Brothers 'world class culinary experience'; and THE FAT DUCK (Tel: 01628 580333) Heston Blumenthal's 'best restaurant in the world'.

ETON and Windsor regard each other across the Thames with what appears to be mutual admiration, and certainly they have the knack of attracting large numbers of visitors, many of whom make it their business to take to the water in one way or another - you have been warned!

Upstream, the river negotiates Boveney Lock, above which a backwater leads from the rear of Bush Ait to Racecourse Yacht Basin and extensive private moorings. Eton College's Dorney Lake is to be a rowing venue for the 2012 Olympics. Boveney Chapel - dedicated to St Mary Magdalene - is cared for by the Friends of Friendless Churches. It dates from the Norman Conquest and largely gleaned its congregation from the ranks of river bargemen.

'Athens' was the sobriquet given to a quiet bathing place on the north bank of the river by generations of Etonians. A commemorative stone recalls one John Lionel Baker, killed in a flying accident in 1917. Boveney Ditch enters the river just upstream of this

point and nowadays carries the county boundary, for Berkshire has 'upped sticks' and requisitioned Eton and Slough since the crass and uncalled for re-organisations of the mid-nineteen-seventies. Royal Windsor is a rare example of a 'figure of eight' racecourse. On race days punters find that the most expedient means of reaching the grandstand is by river bus!

Clewer church overlooks the old mill stream, its churchyard containing the grave of Sir Daniel Gooch, the Great Western Railway's first Locomotive Superintendent. Equally of interest is the bowstring bridge which carries the line from Slough, for it is Brunel's work and dates from 1849. Both the Great Western and London & South Western railway companies had sought to serve Royal Windsor and win Victoria's seal of approval but Eton College had demurred, convinced that vulgar railways would undermine their pupil's morals.

Towered over by the regal outlines of the world famous castle, the Thames arcs equally royally by Eton on its north bank and Windsor to the south. The elegant cast

For facilities at Datchet turn to page 77

iron (and pedestrianised) bridge which links them dates from 1824, and when we last passed beneath, a Caucasian busker stood upon it balefully singing the blues - perhaps, one wag (with an encylopaedic knowlege of Scottish rock music) suggested his name was Fergus. Some fine looking restaurants abut the riverbank and it becomes difficult to resist the temptation to eat, drink and be if not necessarily merry, at least temporarily less morose.

Romney Lock hides itself away from all the razzmatazz. The lock-cottage is demurely whitewashed and dates from 1919. There are glimpses past soaring poplars of Eton College Chapel. Black Potts railway bridge was originally designed by Joseph Locke and of considerably more ornate appearance than now. Neither can much aesthetic virtue be attached to the 1967 rebuilt version of Victoria Bridge. With stern injunctions not to moor along the Royal banks of The Home Park, the Thames flows down past Datchet's pleasant river frontage and a busy boatyard and hire base.

Eton (Map 37)

An insubstantial town of great charm based on a handsome and lengthy High Street.

Eating & Drinking

HOUSE ON THE BRIDGE - Windsor Bridge. Tel: 01753 860914. Smart restaurant with grandstand views of the river.

ANTICO - High Street. Tel: 01753 863977. Plush Italian.

WATERMAN'S ARMS - Brocas Street. Tel: 01753 861001. CAMRA recommended local adjoining Eton College Boat House. Fresh fish daily from Billingsgate.

STROK'S - High Street. Tel: 01753 852359. Twin establishment of Strok's in Windsor, here ensconced within the Christopher Hotel. Excellent (and comparatively inexpensive) bar food; Eton bangers and mash, fish & chips, sandwiches etc.

HENRY VI - High Street. Tel: 01753 866051. Well-appointed pub with secret garden!

Shopping

A branch of Coutts Bank sets the tone for Eton's exclusive High Street, an aura intensified by a quintet of gentlemen's outfitters with prominent displays of the College's uniforms and sports attire within their gilded windows. Galleries and gift shops rub upstart shoulders with such illustrious establishments; groceries and provisions are supplied by Tudor Stores, established at the end of the 18th Century. There is also a pharmacy who double as wine merchants, and an antiquarian bookshop. Look out for the elegant, fluted pillar box on the right hand side of the High Street as you walk away from the Thames.

Things to Do

ETON COLLEGE - High Street. Tel: 01753 671177. Open to the general (disadvantaged) public between Easter and the end of September; though afternoons only during term time. A thought-provoking insight into the history of Britain's most famous school and the lifestyle of its present-day pupils, numbering a startling thirteen hundred or so boys. The College Chapel is worth the entry fee alone.

Connections

TRAINS - see Windsor.

Windsor (Map 37)

Hardly anything about Windsor seems real - half Walt Disney, half Truman Show - and yet it attracts tourists from all over the globe; and, judging by the demeanour of some, even further afield. At the height of the tourist season, and when the flag flies over the battlements, you could be forgiven suspecting that Her Majesty is the only English person left in Windsor.

Eating & Drinking

STROK'S - Thames Street. Tel: 01753 442422. Sophisticated dining within the premises of Sir Christopher Wren's House Hotel. Al Fresco opportunities overlooking the river.

DON BENI - Thames Street. Tel: 01753 622042. Vibrant Italian where you feel part of the cooking experience.

TRE - Thames Street. Tel: 01753 860060. Family run contemporary Italian with attentive service and inexpensive set-course lunches.

LATINO - Church Lane. Tel: 01753 857711. Greek taverna with lovely outdoor tables placed on the cobblestones of Church Lane.

Shopping

Peascod Street slopes down from the castle walls and boasts the main chain stores - Boots, Marks & Spencer, Woolworths et al. Here as well you'll come upon NAUTICALIA, a branch of the outfit at Shepperton - Map 40, who deal in maritime-themed gifts. The WINDSOR ROYAL SHOPPING mall is based around the grandiose Central railway station enlarged in 1897 to mark Victoria's Jubilee.

Things to Do

TOURIST INFORMATION - Central railway station. Tel: 01753 743900 www.windsor.gov.uk Curiously reticent TIC whose staff lurk behind the grilles of the old station booking hall.

continued on page 77

LIVING up to its billing as 'liquid history', the Thames flows past Runnymede and Magna Carta Island as it makes its way down from Datchet to Egham. Bad King John's run-in with the barons in 1215 might all seem like a long time ago, but the Magna Carta set precedents which still impact upon the rights of freemen throughout the democratic world.

Albert Bridge marks the southern extend of Windsor Old Park. Its elegant, balustraded profile heralds the entrance to the New Cut, dug in 1822 to obviate an extravagant bend in the river. In truth this short-cut is rather charmless, so one welcomes the advent of Old Windsor Lock, presided over by a brick-built keeper's cottage dating from 1928.

Between the tail of Old Windsor Lock and Friary Island on the east bank of the river stands Honeypot Cottage, a quaint thatched building with three conical roofs. For many years it belonged to the much loved actress Beryl Reid and her feline retinue. The Thames here is broad and there are a number of boat-filled backwaters. Dutch barge disease appears to be spreading!

When Jerome K. Jerome alluded to the Bells of Ouseley (sic) in *Three Men In A Boat*, he was not to know that it would be hit by a German V2 rocket half a century later: it is now a Harvester restaurant. The eponymous bells are reputed to have been mislaid in the river hereabouts as they were being secretly conveyed from Osney Abbey at Oxford by monks anxious that they should be saved from Henry VIII at the time of the Dissolution.

Half a mile downstream lies French Brothers boatyard. You may be fortunate enough to catch a glimpse here of

STAINES

WINDSOR

37

Ham Island
sewage works

Wraysbury

New Cut

Weirs !

Albert Bridge

Weir !

Old Windsor Lock*
5ft 9ins
Tel: 01753 861822

Friary Island

Old Windsor

B3021

Bells of Ouzeley

French

Lutyens Lodges

Magna Carta Island

Ankerwicke Priory

Salters

Magna Carta Memorial

A328

John F. Kennedy Memorial

Runnymede

B376

Bell Weir Lock*
6ft 0ins
Tel: 01784 432333

Weir !

The Island

A308

A30

Holm Island

3

STAINES

Egham

M25

VIRGINIA WATER

Nuneham, a former Salters steamer, built by Clarkes of Brimscombe on the Thames & Severn Canal in 1898. She was converted to diesel propulsion after the Second World War and subsequently passed out of Salters fleet, eventually being acquired by French Brothers and beautifully restored to steam to mark her centenary.

French Brothers landing stage offers access to Runnymede Meadows, under the aegis now of the National Trust. Refreshments are obtainable at one of the Lutyens designed lodges or kiosks. Within easy walking distance of the riverbank are two memorials with American connotations: the Magna Carta Memorial was erected in 1957 by the American Bar Association as a symbol of freedom under law; eight years later, and less than a fortnight after the assassination of John F. Kennedy in Dallas, the British Government gifted an acre of land at Runnymede to the U.S.A. as a mark of respect in his memory. A third monument rises conspicuously above a wooded hillside to the south-west in the form of a clock tower built in 1952 and containing within its walls a sad roll call of some twenty thousand missing Commonwealth airmen.

As it flows past Runnymede, the Thames forms the boundary between Berkshire and Surrey. The keen as mustard members of Wraysbury Skiff and Punting Club put their elegant craft through their paces on this reach of the river. Bell Weir Lock lies adjacent to the notorious M25 and the traffic noise rarely dissipates. There are two bridges - arch rivals you could say - that nearest the lock having been designed by Lutyens, though erected posthumously in 1961.

continued from page 75
WINDSOR CASTLE - Castle Hill. Tel: 0207 766 7304 *www.royalcollection.org.uk* 'The oldest and largest occupied castle in the world.' CITY SIGHTSEEING - open top bus tours encompassing both Windsor and Eton. Tel: 0871 666 0000 *www.city-sightseeing.com*
Connections
TRAINS - First Great Western link with Slough from Central; South-West Trains link with Datchet, Staines and Waterloo from Riverside. Tel: 08457 484950.

Datchet (Map 37)
Public moorings render this a useful stopping-off point for those genetically-programmed to shy away from the excesses of Windsor. Over the railway level-crossing you'll find a couple of pubs and an Italian restaurant (PICCOLA VENEZIA - Tel: 01753 549314), two sandwich bars and two off-licences. There's no general store as such, but there is a good butcher, a newsagent and a pharmacy. Trains run to Windsor & Eton Riverside, Staines and London Waterloo.

Old Windsor lock

Hampton Cour

Romney Lock, Windsor
78

Richmond
riverfront

AT its most bourgeois, the Thames slips through Staines, fulfilling the subliminal maritime fantasies of thousands of riparian dwellers. The River Colne, a confidant of Grand Union canallers, enters the Thames just below Staines Bridge, the work of Sir John Rennie, son of the more widely known canal engineer and bridge and dock builder. Here the riverside has been municipally enhanced to good effect and there are handy free moorings, whilst youngsters get a good grounding in the theories and practices of rowing. Below the railway bridge (adorned with yellow sight lines to prevent swans from flying into its unforgiving grey girders) a lych gate gives off the towpath into St Peter's Church, endowed by Sir Edward Clark KC who defended Oscar Wilde. Villas, bungalows and maisonettes characterise the waterside all the way down to Penton Hook, and notwithstanding an obvious disparity in era, an homogeneity is neatly established, near yet far neighbours regarding each other

quizzically across the river where water replaces mere asphalt: one senses that the Thames lends additional subtle shades of character to those fortunate enough to dwell on its banks.

Penton Hook Lock dates from 1814 and lays claim to being the most westerly lock constructed at the behest of the City of London. Framed by horse chestnuts, the keeper's cottage is a pre-Conservancy original. It slices off a positively rococo meander of the river, the downstream portion of which leads to an extensive marina. Opposite Laleham Raw Water Intake, Laleham Boatyard usually boasts a fine array of classic cruisers. The poet Matthew Arnold was born in Laleham and is buried in the churchyard. His almost equally famous father taught here before moving to Rugby School in 1828. Another well known Laleham family are the Lucans: one of them gave the disastrously misleading order which led to the Charge of the Light Brigade; another was a prominent activist in the early days of the Inland Waterways Association; and a third effected a celebrated disappearance.

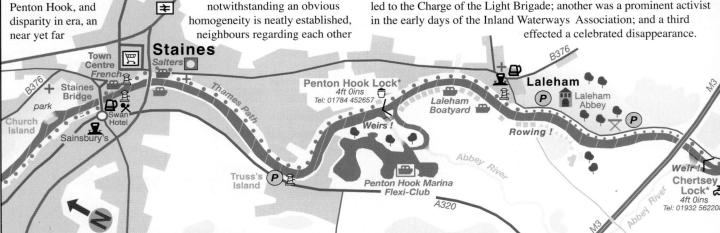

Staines (Map 39)

The malodorous linoleum works is long gone, remembered solely by the charming statue of two men carrying a roll of the stuff along the High Street. On the wall of the elegant, Italianate Town Hall (now a Smith & Jones pub) a plaque commemorates Staines's cameo role in the Battle of Trafalgar. Nelson's victory was achieved on 21st October 1805, but it took sixteen days for that news to reach the Admiralty in London. First by way of the schooner *Pickle* which docked at Falmouth on 4th November, thence by a post-chaise which took 37 hours to cover the 271 miles. It's horses were changed 21 times en route, the penultimate change taking place at Staines on the evening of 5th November. A footnote in history, for sure, but an interesting item of trivia which encapsulates this proud little riverside borough's pedigree which is traceable back to Roman times.

Eating & Drinking

THE SWAN HOTEL - The Hythe. Tel: 01784 452494. Congenial Fullers (of Chiswick) pub with customer moorings and patio overlooking river. Food and accommodation.
SAFFRON - The Hythe. Tel: 01784 459717. Contemporary Indian across the street.
MAMA MIA - Clarence Street. Tel: 01784 454911. Cosy Italian within easy reach of the public moorings.
THAMES LODGE HOTEL - riverside between bridges. Tel: 01784 464433. Bar & grill open to non-residents. Customer mooring.
STAINES STEAK HOUSE - High Street. Tel: 01784 451181. Retro grill beyond the railway bridge.

Shopping

An unexpectedly sophisticated shopping venue with two shopping malls, an imposing Debenhams, Marks & Spencer and a cheerfully pedestrianised High Street which continues to a coda beyond the railway.

Connections

TRAINS - frequent services to/from London Waterloo and Reading, plus junction for Windsor & Eton Riverside. Tel: 08457 484950.
BUSES - throughout Surrey, but specifically to Shepperton for Thames-pathers. Tel: 0870 608 2 608.
TAXIS - Blue Star Cars. Tel: 01784 465656.

Laleham (Map 39)

Public moorings render this otherwise innocuous village worth considering as a stopping point with easy access to a convenience store and a pub called The Three Horseshoes. Some handsome Georgian and neo-Georgian houses adorn the village green, persuading you that you are much deeper into the countryside.

Hampton Court (Map 41)

Riverside tourist honeypot which positively hooches with visitors from all over the world all summer through. Nice walks to be enjoyed in Bushy Park where the deer tamely graze as you pass within touching distance.

Eating & Drinking

LE PETIT NANTAIS - Bridge Road. Tel: 020 8979 2309. Terrific little French restaurant on the south bank of the river; a real 'find'! Quelquefois un accordeon accompagner votre repast.
RIVER'S EDGE BRASSERIE - Tel: 020 8979 9988. Good customer moorings (north bank immediately upstream of bridge) make this hotel annex a favourable choice for boaters. Fine riverside terrace for al fresco meals.

Shopping

The homely Hampton Court Superstore caters for most foody needs and there's a butcher a little further along Bridge Road as well. Otherwise the emphasis is on antiques, galleries, gifts and high fashion.

Things to Do

HAMPTON COURT PALACE - Tel: 0870 752 7777 *www.hrp.org.uk* Sumptuous Tudor palace surrendered by Cardinal Wolsey to Henry VIII. Good public moorings on the North bank downstream of Hampton Court Bridge provide easy access.

Connections

TRAINS - terminus of outer suburban services to/from London Waterloo. Tel: 08457 484950.
BUSES - useful riparian links for Thames-pathers with Kingston and Walton. Tel: 0870 608 2 608.

Thames Ditton (Map 41)

Weatherboarded cottages and a flint church lend a Kentish feel to this peaceful enclave, especially when you discover that one of the best pubs is serving Shepherd Neame ales from Faversham. A shame, then, that there are not more mooring options.

Eating & Drinking

YE OLDE SWAN - Summer Road. Tel: 020 8398 1814. A mooring jetty is thoughtfully provided for boating customers by the suspension bridge which links Thames Ditton Island to the outside world. Roomy pub dating from the 13th Century where Henry VIII came to repair for a quiet pint between nuptials. Home made bar and restaurant food. Greene King and Old Speckled Hen beers.
THE ALBANY - Queens Road. Tel: 020 8972 9163. Stylish riverside eating house with theatrical origins adjacent to Dittons Skiff & Punting Club premises. Mooring jetty.

Shopping

Two small delis, a bakery/sandwich bar and greengrocer, post office and newsagent.

Connections

TRAINS - see Hampton Court.

CHERTSEY BRIDGE is finely proportioned and downstream of it the river arcs past Dumsey Meadow where cattle still graze in the time-honoured manner and where wildflowers flourish unimpeded by artificial fertilizers. Opposite Chertsey Meads a small community of houseboats catches the eye. Those who live on Pharaoh's Island commute by dinghy to landing stages on the banks of what passes for civilisation. The islet's name derives from the Battle of the Nile and a good number of its properties bear Egyptian inspired names.

A complex network of waterways surrounds Shepperton Lock, prime amongst which is the River Wey and its Navigation, navigable for some nineteen miles through Surrey (at its most leafy) to the market town of Godalming, four miles upstream of Guildford. At the tail of the lock a ferry operates throughout the summer months, not least for the benefit of those pacing out the Thames Path who, throughout the winter, must otherwise deviate away from the water's edge on something of a trudge through Shepperton village and Lower Halliford. D'Oyly Carte Island once belonged to the impresario Richard D'Oyly Carte, and on it he built the now rather elegantly faded Eyot House - Gilbert & Sullivan being frequent visitors.

Desborough Cut or Channel opened in 1935 to save some three-quarters of a mile, though the original course of the river remains equally navigable, and rendered perhaps more attractive for those not in a rush by virtue of the pubs on its banks. The two routes rejoin each other just upstream of Walton Bridge, a hideous and supposedly 'temporary' Bailey bridge since being damaged in the Second World War, but long earmarked for rebuilding as an imposing bowspring girder

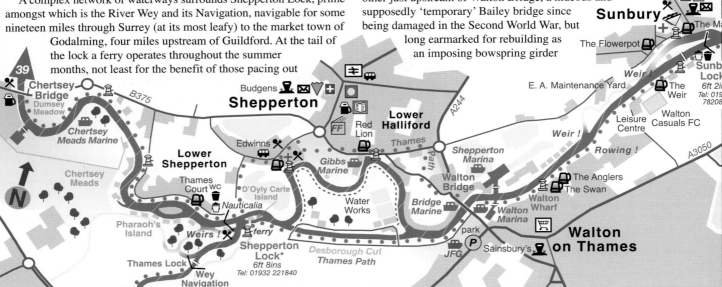

structure. Both Canaletto and Turner had painted its earlier manifestations, but this present monster would challenge any landscape artist to render it picturesque. Two busy marinas and a boatyard create additional levels of boating activity as the river makes its way down Walton Reach through a world of bungalows and riverside chalets bewildering in their invention and individuality. The Environment Agency, who nowadays are responsible for upkeep of the river, have a sizeable maintenance yard and drydock on the approach to Sunbury. Sunbury Locks are paired, but it is usually the southernmost (on the right heading downstream) which is used today, its older partner being still hand-operated. Like Penton Hook, it retains a pre-Thames Conservancy lock-keeper's house. On this occasion, however, a newer house, dated 1959, has supplanted the original.

Shepperton (Map 40)

Famous for its film studios which are located near the giant Queen Mary Reservoir a couple of miles to the north of the river. Lower Shepperton is quaint and centred on the ancient parish church of St Nicholas. Shepperton proper is pragmatically suburban.

Eating & Drinking

WARREN LODGE HOTEL - Church Square. Tel: 01932 242972. Bar & restaurant meals for non-residents.
BLUBECKERS & EDWINNS - Church Square. Tel: 01932 243377. Doyen of the sophisticated restaurant chain formed in 1977 - see also Harefield in *Pearson's Canal Companion to the Oxford & Grand Union Canals*.
THAMES COURT - riverside above Shepperton Lock. Tel: 01932 221957. All day family pub.

Shopping

No shops in Lower Shepperton by the river, but good facilities in Shepperton itself to the north of the B375 about quarter of an hour away. NAUTICALIA'S gift shop and chandlery lies adjacent to the lock. Tel: 01932 244396.

Connections

TRAINS - terminus of outer suburban branch line from London Waterloo. Tel: 08457 484950.
BUSES - service 438 operates hourly, Mon-Sat, between Shepperton railway station and Staines via Laleham. Tel: 0870 608 2 608.

Walton on Thames (Map 40)

The town centre is of blandly Sixties aspect, but the riverside is much more charming and traditional: the musical half of Gilbert & Sullivan lived at River House; elephants disembarked from barges to join travelling circuses at Walton Wharf; and (with flagrant disregard of local bye-laws) Julius Caesar forded the river here in 54BC.

Eating & Drinking

THE ANGLERS - riverside by Walton Wharf. Tel: 01932 223996. Popular waterside hostelry. Adnams, Charles Wells and guest beers.
THE SWAN - Manor Row. Tel: 01932 225964. Sprawling Young's pub offering home-cooked pub food. Jerome (*Smoke Gets In Your Eyes*) Kern wooed and won the landlord's daughter here in 1910.
THE WEIR - Waterside Drive. Tel: 01932 782078. Riverside pub adjacent to Sunbury Lock channel and Walton Casuals Football Club. Badger beers from Blandford Forum.

Shopping

All the 'High Street' brands lurk in the town centre less than ten minutes walk from moorings at Walton Wharf. Large branch of Sainsbury's.

Connections

TRAINS - the railway station lies a lengthy hike to the south of the town centre. If you get that far you'll find frequent trains to/from Waterloo. Tel: 08457 484950.

BUSES - links with Shepperton and Kingston might come to the aid of one-way walkers. Tel: 0870 608 2 608.

Sunbury on Thames (Map 40)

Echoes Shepperton in that it is at its prettiest beside the river, and good public moorings - approached from below Sunbury Lock - encourage waterborne visitors. A walled garden can be explored with time at one's disposal.

Eating & Drinking

THE FLOWERPOT HOTEL - Thames Street. Tel: 01932 780741. Charming Brakspear pub offering food and accommodation.
THE MAGPIE - Thames Street. Tel: 01932 782024. Greene King pub with riverside terrace and mooring jetty. Original meeting place of the Grand Order of Water Rats (the showbiz charity organisation) in 1889. The Magpie was a trotting pony in Newcastle-on-Tyne; it's a long story ...
MOON IN MOON - The Avenue. Tel: 01932 789500. Chinese restaurant.

Shopping

Useful facilities on The Avenue within easy reach of the public moorings include a small Budgens supermarket, post office, newsagent and pharmacy.

Connections

TRAINS - stop on the Shepperton branch. Tel: 08457 484950.

THE Thames flows down past Sunbury through a glittering landscape of reservoirs and water works dating from the mid-19th Century, prior to which much of the capital's drinking water was extracted from the Thames and, given the fact that it also functioned as a receptacle for sewage, cholera was not surprisingly rife. Sunbury Court was built in the 18th Century and in recent years has been used as a conference centre. It lends its name to an island which boasts an agglomeration of chalets and bungalows, the first in a procession of 'islands in the stream' which capture your attention and engage your curiosity in almost equal measure. Platt's Eyot was the location of Thorneycroft's boatbuilding yard, its dilapadated

corrugated-iron erecting sheds bear melancholy witness to a heyday which had its zenith during the First World War when motor torpedo boats were constructed here for the Admiralty. Fortunately, Molesey Lock was capacious enough to accept such vessels, having already been lengthened (to a whopping 268 feet in 1906) for the upstream coal traffic to Port Hampton. The discharged cargoes of coal were transported to the pumping stations at Hampton and Kempton (better known, of course, for its race course, just off-map) by a narrow gauge railway. Much of its two foot line remains in situ and there are hopes that it may one day be resurrected as a tourist attraction. Canal aficionados may be interested to learn that its fleet of three steam locomotives hailed from the Kerr Stuart works at Stoke on Trent where L. T. C. Rolt was apprenticed.

Prominent on the riverside stands Garrick's Shakespeare Temple, erected by the acclaimed 18th Century actor in

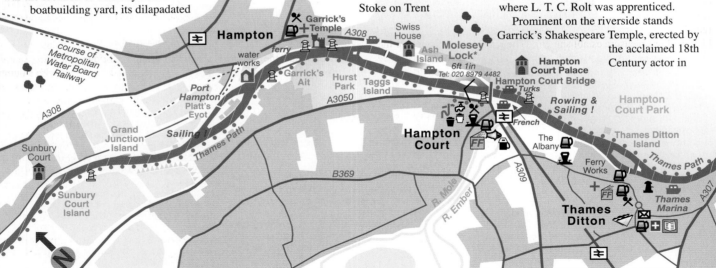

For details of facilities at Hampton Court and Thames Ditton turn to page 81

1773 in honour of the bard. David Garrick purchased Hampton House in 1754 and had it rebuilt by Robert Adam. Level with Garrick's Ait on the Surrey bank stood Hurst Park Race Course which featured memorably in *Nicholas Nickleby*. One of its grandstands was burnt down by suffragettes in 1913. Upon closure of the course in 1962 its last grandstand was sold to Mansfield Town FC!

Garrick's Temple and "Astoria"

Tagg's Island, now host to an eclectic flotilla of characterful houseboats, was once the base of the impresario Fred Karno who operated a number of crowd-pleasing attractions on the islet. It was he who shipped over a complete Swiss house and had it re-erected on the Middlesex bank. It remains intact, seemingly immune to the vicissitudes of property, unlike his grandiose pleasure establishment, 'The Karsino', a magnet for the rich, famous and libidinous. A colourful character - who, had he lived today, would rarely have been absent from the front covers of *Hello* - Karno is variously attributed as the originator of the custard pie routine, the casting couch and the mentor of Charlie Chaplin. The chaotic, slapstick routines which he encouraged his music hall acts to adopt gave rise to the term 'Fred Karno's Army', a title also adapted for an irreverant song sung by the troops in the trenches.

At the height of his success, Karno had an elegant houseboat built for him by a boatyard in Brentford. Launched in 1913, it was called *Astoria*, and cost a cool million in today's values. Thirteen years later he was bankrupt and ownership passed to Vesta Victoria, the comedienne who sang *Daddy Wouldn't Buy Me A Bow Wow*. Nowadays, fully restored to pristine condition, it belongs to Dave Gilmour of Pink Floyd and is used as an unlikely recording studio. Pink Floyd's albums *A Momentary Lapse of Reason* and *The Division Bell* along with Gilmour's own appropriately titled *On an Island* were all recorded on *Astoria*.

The civilised world is polarised into those who think of Hampton Court Palace in terms of Cardinal Wolsey and those for whom it conjures images of Harris and his chums' experience of the famous maze, as so deliciously described in *Three Men In A Boat*. Whichever set claims you, there is no escaping the Palace's impact on the river traveller. Hampton Court Bridge was designed by Sir Edward Lutyens and opened ceremoniously in 1933 by the Prince of Wales, the man who popularised the zip-fly and who was later to briefly become Edward VIII before abdicating the throne for the beguiling charms of Wallis Simpson.

Having risen romantically on the slopes of the Sussex Weald, the River Mole enters the Thames just downstream of the bridge as it glides serenely past Hampton Court Palace. The confluence is a busy spot with a number of 'steamer' piers in the vicinity. Half a mile downstream, the handsome boathouse of the Dittons Skiff & Punting Club stands on the Surrey bank; the club was founded in 1923 and is one of a number on the banks of the Thames still catering for these arcane water sports.

Thames Ditton Island has a permanent population in excess of a hundred souls. Chalets and shanties began popping up on it early in the 20th Century, but it didn't have a permanent link to the rest of the world until a pedestrian suspension bridge joined it with the Surrey bank just before the Second World War. Many of the houses have been rebuilt more substantially but a few of the original bungalows remain to remind the island's dwellers of their more humble origins. Ferry Works on the Surrey bank houses various small businesses now, but its past output includes AC Cars and Willans & Robinsons steam reciprocating engines.

T Teddington Locks the Thames loses its freshwater status and becomes tidal. An obelisk, erected in 1909, marks the change in responsibility for navigation between the Thames Conservancy (or these days the Environment Agency) and the Port of London Authority.

Surbiton almost onomatopoeically defines suburbia, though this hardly impinges on the river. Uncharacteristically, L. T. C. Rolt sprang to its defence in his *Thames From Mouth to Source*. Perhaps he was still pumping adrenalin from the sight of Dutch coastal vessels delivering coal (which they had loaded from staithes on the River Tyne and carried down the East Coast) to Kingston Gasworks.

The Italianate tower of St Raphael's Catholic church looms over the riverbank on the approach to Kingston and there is a landing stage for Turks trip boat operations just before the entry of the Hogsmill River. Kingston Bridge dates from 1828 but has been progressively widened to cope with traffic demands. By 1906 it could lay claim to be the first Thames bridge to have trams running over it - would that they still were!

A massive John Lewis department store emphasises Kingston's credentials as a centre for shopping, but intrudes upon the river's propensity for avoiding harsh realities. The remains of a wharf to which tugs hauling trains of coal-laden lighters plied with fuel for the town's since demolished power station recall another example of lost commercial trade, but you only have to look at the adjoining railway bridge to realise that it was the dense network of lines on either bank of the Thames which brought about the demise of river traffic rather than any inherent weakness in the carriage of goods by water. By way of consolation, the railways expedited an explosion in the growth of pleasure traffic on the river. The cast iron railway bridge was built by Thomas Brassey for the London & South Western Railway in 1863. Canbury Gardens provide a soothing environment along the Surrey bank. Here, in less salubrious times, they made

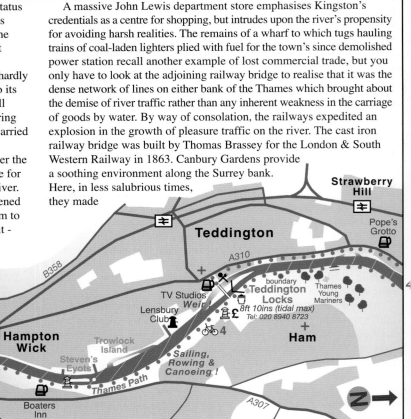

'native guano', or dried human sewage for use as a manure. Inured to its noisome presence, the locals jocularly knew the gardens as 'Perfume Parade'.

The river broadens as it sweeps down to Teddington in a reach made busy by all sorts of boating activities. Lensbury, on the Middlesex bank, is a private club and leisure complex which once belonged exclusively to Shell. A hundred and thirty five miles from Lechlade, Teddington Lock marks the tidal limit of the River Thames. There are three chambers: the massive 'barge' lock dating from 1904 (650ft long x 24ft 9ins wide) which was once used by tug-hauled trains of lighters; the 'launch' lock of 1857 (177ft 11ins x 24ft 4ins); and the 'skiff' lock (49ft 6ins x 5ft 10ins). The locks are manned 24 hours per day, 365 days of the year and the friendly (if frequently busy) keepers are fountains of navigational lore. From the neighbouring Tough's Boatyard a hundred privately owned 'Little Ships' bravely set course for Dunkirk in 1940 to help in the evacuation of the British Expeditionary Force.

Kingston on Thames (Map 42)

Turn a blind eye to the architectural insensitivity of John Lewis's ungainly riverside store, Kingston gets much better than this once you've wended your way down its side streets and come upon the Market Place with its fine Italianate Town Hall and the anachronistic golden statue of Queen Anne. Another alley leads to the Apple Market, whence you can come full circle to Clatten Bridge which spans the Hogsmill River and is thought to derive its name from the sound of horses hooves. Back beside the Thames, the redevelopment of Charter Quay presents a cogent response to previous debacle.

Eating & Drinking

FRERE JACQUES - Riverside Walk. Tel: 020 8546 1332. French restaurant with Thames-side views.
BISHOP OUT OF RESIDENCE - Riverside. Tel: 020 8546 4965. Lively modern all-day Youngs pub serving food from 10am to 10.30pm.
STRADA - Griffin Centre. Tel: 020 8974 8555. Contemporary Italian.
THE BOATERS INN - Canbury Gardens. Tel: 020 8541 4672. Homely riverside bar with limited customer moorings.
ROYAL FISH BAR - Eden Street. Tel: 020 8549 2299. Traditional eat in or take-away fish & chips.

Shopping

Kingston offers excellent and enjoyable shopping facilities which range from the hauteur of Bentalls and John Lewis's department stores to the magnaminity of the Market Square, and these are easily accessed by boaters from good moorings on the Middlesex bank upstream of Kingston Bridge.

Things to Do

TOURIST INFORMATION - Market Place. Tel: 020 8547 5592 www.kingston.gov.uk

Connections

TRAINS - Kingston loop services to/from London Waterloo with useful link with Shepperton for

Kingston-on-Thames

Thames Path walks.
TAXIS - Kingston Black Cab. Tel: 020 8546 1993.

Teddington (Map 42)

Teddington Studios can trace their origins back to the dawn of film-making. Many British feature films were made here in the 1930s, but the studios were destroyed by a V1 rocket in 1944, and did not return to full production until four years later when they were formally re-opened by Danny Kaye. In the Sixties and Seventies the studios enjoyed a heyday in the making of television programmes such as *The Avengers*, *Minder* and *The Benny Hill Show*.

Eating & Drinking

TIDE END COTTAGE - Ferry Road. Tel: 020 8977 7762. Charming Greene King pub easily reached by footbridge from Teddington Lock.
THE ANGLERS - Broom Road. Tel: 020 8977 7475. Popular refurbished inn with large riverside garden. Benny Hill lived on Broom Road!
THE WHARF - Manor road. Tel: 020 8977 6333. Smart bar/restaurant with good views overlooking Teddington Lock.

Connections

TRAINS - Kingston loop services to/from Waterloo with links to Kingston and Richmond. Tel: 08457 484950.

43 LOWER THAMES

EXTENSIVE swathes of parkland accompany the Thames down to Kew Bridge, and but for the continual drone of aircraft on their descent to Heathrow you might almost imagine yourself much farther upstream on an altogether more rurally inclined river. On Eel Pie Island (which gained its name from early river tourists stopping there to taste a local delicacy) there used to be an hotel which became a venue for many early rhythm and blues acts in the 1960s: Long John Baldry, Rod Stewart, David Bowie, The Rolling Stones, The Yardbirds and The Who to name but a few. In an earlier musical era, Kenny Ball and George Melly played jazz there, but following a demolition order, the hotel was mysteriously burned down in 1971.

Hammerton's Ferry was established in 1909. Back then it cost a penny to cross, now it costs a pound, but it is still a great means

of communication between two remarkable properties, Marble Hill and Ham House. The former is the younger by a century, being completed in 1729 at the behest of George II for his mistress, the Countess of Suffolk. Ham House dates from 1610 and belonged to the matrimonially more fastidious Earl of Lauderdale. Marble Hill is open to the general public under the aegis of English Heritage; Ham House the National Trust, and Hammerton's Ferry provides an appropriately old-fashioned means of progressing between the two great houses.

The Thames bends majestically past Glover's Ait overlooked by the imposing Star & Garter home for disabled servicemen. Richmond's riverfront is graciously neo-classical. Its bridge dates from 1777 and is palpably one of the prettiest on the Thames. Given the semi-tidal

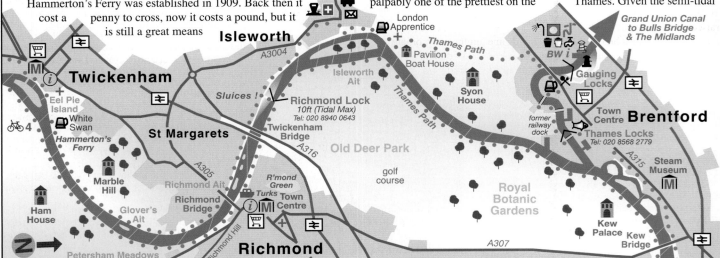

Isleworth

Twickenham

St Margarets

Eel Pie Island

White Swan

Hammerton's Ferry

Marble Hill

Ham House

Glover's Ait

Petersham Meadows

A3004

Sluices !

Richmond Ait

Richmond Bridge

Richmond Hill

Richmond

Turks

R'mond Green

Town Centre

London Apprentice

Thames Path

Pavilion Boat House

Isleworth Ait

Richmond Lock
10ft (Tidal Max)
Tel: 020 8940 0643

Twickenham Bridge

A316

A305

Old Deer Park

golf course

Syon House

Thames Path

former railway dock

Royal Botanic Gardens

A307

Grand Union Canal to Bulls Bridge & The Midlands

BW i

Gauging Locks

Town Centre

Brentford

Thames Locks
Tel: 020 8568 2779

A315

Steam Museum

Kew Palace

Kew Bridge

A307

To Limehouse & the Thames Estuary

status of the Thames at this point, the plying of trip boats, and the rowing boats and skiffs which one can hire, there is a maritime atmosphere about Richmond's elegant river frontage; though, paradoxically, no formal provision for visitor moorings. In common with Black Potts Bridge at Windsor, Richmond railway bridge was designed by Joseph Locke in 1848, and was strengthened sixty years later by the Horseley Iron Works of BCN fame. Cheek by jowl it spans the Thames alongside the ferro-concrete simplicity of Twickenham Bridge, opened by the Prince of Wales on the very same day in 1933 that he cut the tape on the new bridges at Hampton Court (Map 41) and Chiswick - one trusts he had a good attention span!

Controlled by the Port of London Authority, Richmond Lock maintains a minimum depth of water of five feet, nine inches in the reach upstream as far as Teddington. Two hours after High Water, sluices are lowered into the river to create this artifical depth. They remain in place until two hours before the next High Water, and during the intervening period, passing vessels are obliged to use the lock. During the period when the sluices are raised, boats may pass beneath them unhindered. Navigational matters notwithstanding, Richmond Lock is a handsome aggregate of ornate Victorian kiosks and cabins which would not look out of place on the front at Brighton or Eastbourne. As with Teddington, Richmond Lock is manned (in the modern parlance) 'twenty-four/seven'.

Skirting Old Deer Park - where fledgling rugby internationals were played before Twickenham was opened in 1909 - the Thames, now prone to significant fluctuations in level, runs northwards in the direction of Brentford. Two strands of the River Crane enter the Thames at either end of willowy, heron-haunted Isleworth Ait. Laid up lighters recall the lost trades of the tidal river.

The picturesque Pavilion Boat House provides a precursor to Syon House, a stately pile dating largely from the 16th Century with interiors by Robert Adam, and now a hugely popular visitor attraction. Were its gracious demesne not sufficiently alluring, the opposite bank of the Thames skirts the Royal Botanic Gardens at Kew. And so it is by being book-ended between two of Greater London's most revered properties, that our coverage of the Thames comes to its conclusion at Brentford. Downstream lies Kew Bridge, Central London and the sea, but for those voyaging between the river and the canal system, or vice versa, Brentford is a border post which needs to be negotiated with a degree of foresight and care.

Atmospherically, the passage through Brentford has all the makings of a great inland waterway adventure. It is a long time since trains of lighters congregated on the flood tide to pass through Thames Locks and the Gauging Locks on to the Grand Union Canal, but a latent, post-industrial ambience remains, and can palpably be embraced by those in tune with the past; at least as far upstream as the canal basin, for this is now couched in a 21st Century waterscape of apartment blocks, congregated restaurants, and a Holiday Inn hotel. Gauging Locks are an automated pair, boater-operated by a contol panel located on the central island between the two chambers. Above them lie plentiful Visitor Moorings, boater facilities, and a British Waterways information office - Tel: 020 7985 7780. To expedite erudite progress up the Grand Union, acquire a copy of *Pearson's Canal Companion to the Oxford & Grand Union Canals*.

Navigating between Teddington and Brentford

Boaters making their way along the tidal Thames between Teddington Locks and Brentford Gauging Locks need to plan ahead. Thames Locks at Brentford are only open at specific states of the tide and use of them needs to be booked in advance by telephoning 020 8568 2779. British Waterways publish a *Tidal Locks Availability* leaflet twice a year which can be obtained from their Paddington Office - Tel: 020 7985 7200 or email *enquiries.london@britishwaterways.co.uk*

Passage between Teddington and Brentford takes approximately one and a quarter hours and to make the best of the ebb tide you should plan to pass through Teddington Lock half an hour before high water. In the opposite direction plan to leave Brentford about two hours before high water and your passage upstream will have the benefit of the flow. Teddington Lock can be contacted on 020 8940 8723.

Strictly speaking, all craft using the tidal Thames should be equipped with VHF radio. However, canal-based craft travelling solely between Brentford and Teddington are deemed exempt as long as the Port of London authority are advised in advance by telephoning 020 7743 7900.

Richmond upon Thames   (Map 43)

Originally known as Sheen, but renamed by Henry VII after his Dukedom in Yorkshire, Richmond beams so beguilingly down upon the Thames that passing boaters can only be frustrated by the lack of formal visitor moorings. There is much to admire and to enjoy, and land-based visitors can graduate from Richmond Green to Richmond Hill with growing appreciation for a handsome town which should never mistakenly be consigned to oblivion as a mere satellite of the capital.

Eating & Drinking

TIDE TABLES - Richmond Bridge. Tel: 020 8948 8285. Cafe with waterside terrace.

H2O - riverbank just downstream of Richmond Bridge. Tel: 020 8948 0220. Floating restaurant delightfully housed in former Oxford college barge.

WATERMANS ARMS - Water Lane. Tel: 020 8940 2893. Cosy and friendly *Good Beer Guide* recommended Youngs pub with a resident golden retriever called 'Sam'. Inexpensive (by London & SE standards) bar menu and Thai food.

Shopping

Excellent shopping centre with some fine independent retailers. King Street is rich in quirky, off-beat outlets, as are Paved Court and Brewers Lane; the latter playing host to DANIELI's which dispenses freshly-made Italian ice cream.

Things to Do

TOURIST INFORMATION - Old Town Hall. Tel: 020 8940 9125 *www.visitrichmond.co.uk* MUSEUM OF RICHMOND - Old Town Hall. Tel: 020 8332 1141 *www.museumofrichmond.com* RIVER THAMES VISITOR CENTRE - floating visitor centre moored upstream of Richmond Bridge. Tel: 020 8940 7500.

HAM HOUSE - Tel: 020 8940 1950.

MARBLE HILL HOUSE - Tel: 020 8892 5115.

Connections

TRAINS - frequent trains to/from London Waterloo and also the westernmost terminus of the useful North London Line and the District Line. Tel: 08457484950.

Twickenham   (Map 43)

Synonymous with rugby football worldwide, Twickenham away from its burgeoning stadium (hosting the Rolling Stones when we last passed through - far removed from their humble Eel Pie Island origins) resembles a smaller version of Richmond, but similarly lacks formal visitor mooring facilities - though Hammerton's Ferry may be able to squeeze you onto their pontoon at a pinch - Tel: 020 8892 9620.

Eating & Drinking

THE WHITE SWAN - Riverside. Tel: 020 8892 2166. Charming waterside inn with terrace overlooking pebbly 'beach' at low tide.

Shopping

Church Street hosts an array of characterful shops, whilst elsewhere most practical needs are met.

Things to Do

TOURIST INFORMATION - York Street. Tel: 020 8891 7272.

TWICKENHAM MUSEUM - The Embankment. Tel: 020 8408 0070. Local history collections housed in former waterman's cottage. Fascinating displays with much of riverine import. Excellent web-site too: *www.twickenham-museum.org.uk*

Isleworth   (Map 43)

Looks its best from the river and deteriorates the deeper into its hinterland you go.

Eating & Drinking

LONDON APPRENTICE - riverside. Tel: 020 8560 1915. Characterful pub with a lengthy history traceable back to when Henry VIII used it for assignations with Catherine Howard and Charles II with Nell Gwynne. Nice menu (including home-made fishfinger baguettes!) and Fullers London Pride.

Brentford   (Map 43)

Redevelopment marches remorselessly on, but there are pockets of an older (and who's to say not wiser) Brentford, not least The Butts, a charming backwater behind the Market Place.

Eating & Drinking

PREZZO - High Street (overlooking Gauging Locks). Tel: 020 8758 0998. Fast-growing and reliable contemporary Italian chain.

THE WEIR - Market Place. Tel: 020 8568 3600. Formerly a street corner local called The White Horse, this is now a sophisticated bar and eating place with a fine garden backing on to the River Brent. Fascinatingly, the artist Turner stayed here as a boy circa 1785.

Shopping

All facilities in High Street, including a branch of Somerfield.

Things to Do

SYON HOUSE - Tel: 020 8560 0881 *www.syonpark.co.uk* 17th Century home of the Dukes of Northumberland, 5 minutes walk from Gauging Locks and Visitor Moorings. KEW BRIDGE STEAM MUSEUM - Green Dragon Lane. Tel: 020 8568 4757 *www.kbsm.org* Superb museum housed in 19th Century waterworks dominated by ornate tower chimney.

Connections

TRAINS - frequent services to/from London Waterloo and Staines or Windsor, Reading etc. Tel: 08457 484950.

BUSES - frequent buses to all parts of the Greater London compass, though alas no trolleybuses anymore! Tel: 0870 608 2 608.

How to use the Maps

There are forty-three numbered maps whose layout is shown by the Route Planner inside the front cover. Maps 1 to 21 cover the Kennet & Avon between Bristol and Reading; Maps 22 to 43 cover the River Thames between Oxford and Brentford. The maps are easily read in either direction. The simplest way of progressing from map to map is to proceed to the next map numbered from the edge of the map you are on. Figures quoted at the top of each map refer to distance per map, locks per map and average cruising time. An alternative indication of timings from centre to centre can be found on the Route Planner. Obviously, cruising times vary with the nature of your boat and the number of crew, so quoted times should be taken only as an estimate. Neither do times quoted take into account any delays which might occur at lock flights in high season or against strong current conditions on the river sections.

Using the Text

Each map is accompanied by a route commentary, and details of most settlements passed through are given close by. Regular readers will already be familiar with our somewhat irreverent approach. But we 'tell it as we find it', in the belief that the users of this guide will find this attitude more valuable than a strict towing of the tourist publicity line.

Towpath Walking

The simplest way to go canal exploring is on foot. It costs largely nothing and you are free to concentrate on the passing scene; something that boaters are not always at liberty to do. The towpath on the Kennet & Avon Canal is in walkable condition throughout, though inclined to be gluey after rain where it has not been upgraded

Information

for use as a cycleway. Furthermore, in its passage through the Kennet Valley, sections of the towpath can prove impassable at times of flood.

The River Avon Trail follows the Bristol Avon closely between Bristol and Bath. Much of the way it is well-surfaced, though in parts it remains merely a field path unsuitable for cycling: www.riveravontrail.org.uk.

The Thames Path is a 184 mile long distance path following the river from its source in Gloucestershire to the Thames Barrier in East London. Between Oxford and Brentford it mostly follows the old towing path except for one or two places where former ferries have ceased to function: www.nationaltrail.co.uk

Towpath Cycling

Cycling canal towpaths is an increasingly popular activity. At present it is theoretically necessary for cyclists wishing to use towpaths to acquire a free of charge permit from a British Waterways office - see opposite page for appropriate addresses. The Kennet & Avon towpath is utilised as National Cycle Route No.4 between Bath and Devizes and Marsh Benham (just west of Newbury) and Reading (though in the latter case there are one or two diversions away from the towpath) and the surface has been significantly and admirably enhanced with this in mind. Cycling beside the Avon and Thames rivers is not formally encouraged, and the surface of their riverbank towpaths is often unsuitable for bicycling with any degree of comfort.

Boating

Boating on inland waterways is an established, though relatively small, facet of the UK holiday industry. There are over 25,000 privately owned boats registered on the canals, but in addition to these numerous firms offer boats for hire: by the day, for short breaks or weekly.

Most hire craft have all the creature comforts you are likely to expect. In the excitement of planning a boating holiday you may give scant thought to the contents of your hire boat, but at the end of a hard day's boating such matters take on more significance, and a well equipped, comfortable boat, large enough to accommodate your crew with something to spare, can make the difference between a good holiday and an indifferent one. All reputable hire firms give newcomers tuition in boat handling and lock working, and first-timers soon find themselves adapting to the pace of things 'on the cut'.

Navigational Advice

LOCKS are part of the charm of inland waterway cruising, but they can be potentially dangerous environments for children, pets and careless adults. Use of them should be methodical and unhurried, whilst special care should be exercised in rain, frost and snow when slippery hazards abound. We lack space for detailed instructions on lock operation: trusting that if you own your own boat you will, by definition, already be experienced in canal cruising; whilst first-time hire boaters should be given tuition in the operation of locks before they set out.

The locks included in this guide are all of the widebeam variety and capable of accepting two narrowboats side by side. On the Kennet & Avon Canal they are boater operated. Similarly on the River Avon, though usually there are keepers on duty at Netham and Hanham locks.

On the **River Thames** all the locks are mechanised and manned. Their telephone numbers appear on our maps. When waiting to use a lock form an orderly queue at the layby provided. When the lock gates open keep alert for instructions from the keeper who may, for reasons of efficiency and/or safety, require boats to enter the lock in a specific order. Once inside the lock you should secure lines fore and aft, keeping them fairly taut as the level rises or falls. Powered boats should switch their engines off whilst in the lock chamber. It is possible to work through Thames locks when unmanned at your own risk. Locks marked with an asterisk can be power-operated out of hours following instructions clearly posted. We strongly recommend that boaters on the Thames acquire an up to date copy of the Environment Agency's *River Thames User's Guide*.

MOORING on the canals featured in this guide is per usual practice - ie on the towpath side, away from sharp bends, bridge-holes and narrows. An open bollard symbol represents visitor mooring sites, either as designated specifically by British Waterways or, in some cases, as recommended by our personal experience or that of our regular correspondents. Of course, one of the great joys of canal boating has always been the opportunity of mooring wherever (sensibly) you like. In recent years, however, it has become obvious that there are an increasing number of undesirable locations, particularly in urban areas, where mooring is not recommended for fear of vandalism, theft or abuse.

On rivers mooring is usually more problematical, the banks are not always even, there are shallows to contend with, and frequently the riparian rights are privately owned. Thus, cruising the rivers Avon and Thames requires careful planning. We have indicated on the maps the best known sites.

Where these are municipally or privately owned there is often a fee to pay - though not always collected! Overnight mooring is available at many Thames locks at the discretion of the lock-keeper. Boaters should not moor where expressly forbidden, for to do so will only cause aggravation.

CLOSURES (or 'stoppages' in canal parlance) traditionally occur on the inland waterways between November and April, during which time most of the heavy maintenance work is undertaken. Occasionally, however, an emergency stoppage, or perhaps water restriction, may be imposed at short notice, closing part of the route you intend to use. Up-to-date details are normally available from hire bases. Alternatively, British Waterways provide a recorded message for private boaters, the number to ring being: 01923 201402. Information is also available on BW's internet site *www.waterscape.com*

On the River Thames details of maintenance closures can be obtained by telephoning 0845 988 1188 - when prompted press 1 followed by 011132.

Useful Contacts

BRITISH WATERWAYS
South West Waterways, Harbour House, West Quay, Gloucester Docks, Gloucester GL1 2LG. Tel: 01452 318000 *www.waterscape.com* Devizes Office, The Locks, Bath Road, Devizes, Wiltshire SN10 1HB Tel: 01380 722859. *British Waterways operate a central emergency telephone service - Tel: 0800 47 999 47.*
RIVER THAMES
Environment Agency, Kings Meadow House, Kings Meadow Road, Reading RG1 8DQ Tel: 0118 953 5000 *www.visitthames.co.uk* Port of London Authority, Harp Lane, London EC3R 6LB. Tel: 020 7743 7900 *www.portoflondon.co.uk*
BRISTOL HARBOUR
Underfall Yard, Cumberland Road, Bristol BS1 6XG Tel: 0117 903 1484 *www.bristol-city.gov.uk*

The Inland Waterways Association was founded in 1946 to campaign for retention of the canal system. Many routes now open to pleasure boaters may not have been so but for this organisation. They also operate a comprehensive mail order service for inland waterway books, videos and DVDs *www.iwashop.com* Membership details may be obtained from: Inland Waterways Association, PO Box 114, Rickmansworth WD3 1ZY. Tel: 01923 711114 *www.waterways.org.uk*

The Kennet & Avon Canal Trust was formed in 1962 with the object of restoring the canal to full navigation. You can join the Trust by contacting them at: Kennet & Avon Canal Trust, Devizes Wharf, Couch Lane, Devizes, Wilts SN10 1EB. Tel: 01380 721279 *www.katrust.org*

Acknowledgements

Traces of Keith Goss's original research and text remain within and are humbly acknowledged. Brian Collings designed and executed the front cover, the forty-seventh in the series. Toby and Ruth Bryant cruised the Thames and submitted copious notes thereafter. Eden Pearson accompanied the author on many of his research sorties, whilst Karen Tanguy continued to fulfil her thankless task as the author's amanuensis! To all - much thanks and appreciation!

Mapping reproduced by permission of Ordnance Survey (based mapping) on behalf of The Controller of Her Majesty's Stationery Office, Crown copyright 100033032.

Hire Bases

ALVECHURCH BOAT CENTRES - Hilperton Marina, Trowbridge, Kennet & Avon Canal, Map 6. Tel: 0870 835 2525 www.alvechurch.com

ANGLO WELSH WATERWAY HOLIDAYS - Bath, Map 4; Monkton Combe, Map 5. Tel: 0117 304 1122 www.anglowelsh.co.uk

BATH NARROW BOATS - Bath, Kennet & Avon Canal, Map 4. Tel: 01225 447276 www.bath-narrowboats.co.uk

BRIDGE BOATS - Reading, River Thames, Maps 21 & 30. Tel: 0118 959 0346 www.bridgeboats.com

THE BRUCE TRUST - boat hire for the disabled from bases at Gt Bedwyn (Map 13) and Foxhangers (Map 8). Tel: 01672 515498. www.brucetrust.org.uk

CAVERSHAM BOAT SERVICES - Reading, River Thames, Maps 21 & 30. Tel: 0118 957 4323 www.cavershamboatservices.co.uk

COLLEGE CRUISERS - Oxford, Oxford Canal, Map 22. Tel: 01865 554343 www.collegecruisers.com

FLEXI-CLUB - Penton Hook, River Thames, Map 39. Tel: 01932 568772 www.pentonservicecentre.co.uk

FOXHANGERS CANAL HOLIDAYS - Devizes, Kennet & Avon Canal, Map 8. Tel: 01380 828795 www.foxhangers.co.uk

KENNET CRUISES - Burghfield, Kennet & Avon Canal, Map 20. Tel: 0118 987 1115 www.kennetcruises.co.uk

KRIS CRUISERS - Datchet, River Thames, Map 37. Tel: 01753 543930 www.kriscruisers.co.uk

READING MARINE - Aldermaston Wharf, Kennet & Avon Canal, Map 19. Tel: 0118 971 3666 www.readingmarine.co.uk

SALLY BOATS - Bradford-on-Avon, Kennet & Avon Canal, Map 5. Tel: 01225 864923 www.sallyboats.ltd.uk

SWANCRAFT - Benson, River Thames, Map 26. Tel: 01491 836700.

WHITE HORSE BOATS - Devizes, Kennet & Avon Canal, Map 8. Tel: 01380 728504 www.whitehorseboats.co.uk

Boatyards

ABINGDON BOAT CENTRE - Abingdon, River Thames, Map 27. Tel: 01235 521125.

BATH MARINA - Newbridge, River Avon, Map 3. Tel: 01225 424301.

BETTER BOATING - Reading, River Thames, Maps 21 & 30. Tel: 0118947 9536.

BOURNE END MARINA - Bourne End, River Thames, Map 35. Tel: 01628 522813.

BRAY MARINA - Bray, River Thames, Map 36. Tel: 01628 623654.

BRIDGE MARINE - Shepperton, River Thames, Map 40. Tel: 01932 245126.

BRISTOL BOATS - Saltford Lock, River Avon, Map 3. Tel: 01225 872032.

BUSHNELLS - Wargrave, River Thames, Map 31. Tel: 0118 940 2162.

BRISTOL MARINA - Bristol, River Avon, Map 1. Tel: 0117 921 3198.

CHERTSEY MEADS MARINE - Chertsey, River Thames, Map 40. Tel: 01932 564699.

D. B. MARINE - Cookham, River Thames, Map 35. Tel: 01628 526032.

DEVIZES MARINA - Devizes, Kennet & Avon Canal, Map 8. Tel: 01380 725300.

FOXHANGERS WHARF - Foxhangers, Kennet & Avon Canal, Map 8. Tel: 01380 828254

FROUDS BRIDGE MARINA - Aldermaston, Kennet & Avon Canal, Map 18. Tel: 0118 971 4508.

GIBBS MARINE - Shepperton, River Thames, Map 40. Tel: 01932 242977.

GIBSON'S BOAT SERVICES - Honey Street, Kennet & Avon Canal, Map 10. Tel: 01672 851232.

HARLEYFORD MARINA - Harleyford, River Thames, Map 34. Tel: 01628 471361 .

HOBBS & SONS - Henley on Thames, River Thames, Map 32. Tel: 01491 572035 .

HILPERTON MARINA - Hilperton, Kennet & Avon Canal, Map 6. Tel: 01225 765243.

NEWBURY BOAT COMPANY - Newbury, Kennet & Avon Canal, Map 16. Tel: 01635 42884.

PENTON HOOK MARINA - Penton Hook, River Thames, Map 39. Tel: 01932 568681.

PORTAVON MARINA - Keynsham, River Avon, Map 2. Tel: 0117 986 1626.

READING MARINE - Tilehurst, River Thames, Map 22. Tel: 0118 942 3877.

SALTFORD MARINA - Saltford, River Avon, Map 3. Tel: 01225 872226.

SHEPPERTON MARINA - Shepperton, River Thames, Map 40. Tel: 01932 243722.

SHERIDAN MARINE - Moulsford, River Thames, Map 27. Tel: 01491 652085.

SOMERSET COAL CANAL COMPANY - Monkton Coombe, Kennet & Avon Canal, Map 5. Tel: 01225 722069.

THAMES DITTON MARINA - Thames Ditton, River Thames, Map 41. Tel: 020 8398 6159.

THAMES & KENNET MARINAS - Caversham, River Thames, Maps 21 & 30. Tel: 0118 948 2911.
WALTON MARINA - Walton, River Thames, Map 40. Tel: 01932 226305.

Day Boat Hire
ABINGDON BOAT CENTRE - Abingdon, River Thames, Map 24. Tel: 01235 521125.
BATH NARROW BOATS - Bath, Kennet & Avon Canal, Map 4. Tel: 01225 447276.
CAVERSHAM BOAT SERVICES - Reading, River Thames, Maps 21 & 30. Tel: 0118 957 4323.
CHERTSEY MEADS MARINE - Chertsey, River Thames, Map 40. Tel: 01932 564699.
DBH MARINE - Walton, River Thames, Map 40. Tel: 01483 224229.
DEVIZES MARINA - Devizes, Kennet & Avon Canal, Map 8. Tel: 01380 725300.
DITTON CRUISERS - Thames Ditton, River Thames, Map 41. Tel: 020 8398 2119.
DUNDAS ENTERPRISES - Brassknocker Basin, Kennet & Avon Canal, Map 5. Tel: 01225 722292.
GREENHAM CANAL SERVICES - Newbury, Kennet & Avon Canal, Map 16. Tel: 01635 31672.
HOBBS - Henley, River Thames, Map 32. Tel: 01491 572035.
HAMPTON FERRY - Hampton, River Thames, Map 41. Tel: 020 8979 7471.
HARTS CRUISERS - Surbiton, River Thames, Map 42. Tel: 020 8398 2119.
KENNET CRUISES - Burghfield, Kennet & Avon Canal, Map 20. Tel: 0118 987 1115.
KRIS CRUISERS - Datchet, River Thames, Map 37. Tel: 01753 543930.
JOHN LOGIE MOTORBOATS - Windsor, River Thames, Map 37. Tel: 07774 983809.
LOCK INN - Bradford-on-Avon, Map 5. Tel: 01255

868068.
RICHMOND BOAT HIRE - Richmond, River Thames, Map 43. Tel: 020 8948 8270.
SWANCRAFT - Benson, River Thames, Map 25. Tel: 01491 836700.
TRANQUIL BOATS - Semington, Kennet & Avon Canal, Map 9. Tel: 01380 870654.
WHITE HORSE BOATS - Devizes, Kennet & Avon Canal, Map 8. Tel: 01380 728504.

Skiff Hire
RICHMOND BOAT HIRE - Richmond, River Thames, Map 43. Tel: 020 8948 82.
THAMES SKIFF HIRE - Walton-on-Thames. Tel: 01932 232433 www.skiffhire.com

Punt Hire
BATH BOATING STATION - Bath, River Avon, Map 4. Tel: 01225 466407.
CHERWELL BOAT HOUSE - Magdelan Bridge, Oxford, River Cherwell, Map 22. Tel: 01865 515978 www.cherwellboathouse.co.uk
SALTERS - Folly Bridge, Oxford, River Thames, Map 22. Tel: 01865 243421 www.salterssteamers.co.uk

Trip Boats
BARBARA McLELLAN - trips from Bradford-on-Avon. Tel: 01225 868683 www.katrust.org
BRISTOL FERRY - scheduled services between Temple Quay and Cumberland Basin. Tel: 0117 927 3416 www.bristolferry.com
BRISTOL PACKET - boat trips around the Floating Harbour and on the River Avon. Tel: 0117 926 8157 www.bristolpacket.co.uk
FRENCH BROTHERS - scheduled boat trips

on various sections of the River Thames. Tel: 01753 851900 www.boat-trips.co.uk
HOBBS OF HENLEY - trips on the Thames at Henley. Tel: 01491 572035 www.hobbs-of-henley.com
JGF PASSENGER BOATS - scheduled services around Walton and Shepperton on the River Thames. Tel: 01932 253374.
JOHN RENNIE - trips along the Kennet & Avon from Sydney Wharf, Bath. Tel: 01225 447276.
JUBILEE - trips from Brassknocker Basin, Monkton Combe. Tel: 01373 813957.
KENNET CRUISES - trips along the Kennet & Avon Canal between Burghfield and Reading. Tel: 0118 987 1115.
KENNET HORSE BOAT - trips aboard the motor vessel *Avon* from Newbury Wharf and aboard the horse-drawn vessel *Kennet Valley* from Kintbury. Tel: 01488 658866. **PEWSEY WHARF CANAL CHARTERS -** trips from Pewsey Wharf. Tel: 01672 564020.
PULTENEY CRUISES - Bath, River Avon, Map 4. Tel: 01225 312900 www.bathboating.com
PRIDE OF BATH - from North Parade Bridge, Bath. Tel: 01225 331647.
ROSE OF HUNGERFORD - boat trips from Hungerford Wharf. Tel: 01488 683389.
SALTERS - scheduled services between Oxford - Abingdon - Wallingford - Reading - Henley - Marlow - Windsor - Staines. Tel: 01865 243421 www.salterssteamers.co.uk
THAMES RIVERCRUISE - trips from Reading to Beale Park. Tel: 0118 948 1088 www.thamesrivercruise.co.uk
TURK LAUNCHES - scheduled services between Richmond, Kingston and Hampton Court on the River Thames. Tel: 020 8546 2434

Nine Good Reasons for Exploring the Canals with Pearsons

8th edition - ISBN 978 0 9 5491168 3

8th edition - ISBN 0 9549116 0 1

7th edition - ISBN 0 9549116 3 6

7th edition - ISBN 0 9545383 8 2

6th edition - ISBN 0 9549116 5 2

7th edition - ISBN 978 0 9 549 1166 9

6th edition - ISBN 0 9549116 2 8

3rd edition - ISBN 0 9545383 4 X

2nd edition - ISBN 978 0 9 5491167 6

Pearson's Canal Companions are published by Central Waterways Supplies. They are widely available from hire bases, boatyards, canal shops, good bookshops, via the internet and the Inland Waterways Association. For further details contact CWS on 01788 546692 or sales@centralwaterways.co.uk